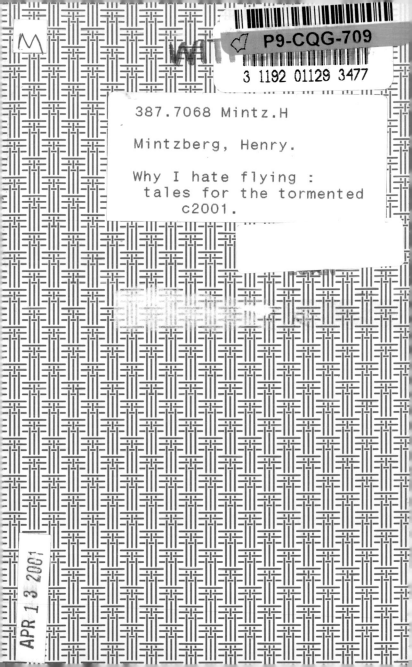

WHY I
HATE
FLYING

WHY I HATE FLYING

TALES FOR THE TORMENTED TRAVELER

HENRY MINTZBERG

TEXERE

New York   London

Published by

TEXERE LLC
55 East 52nd Street
New York, NY 10055

Tel: +1 (212) 317 5106
Fax: +1 (212) 317 5178
www.etexere.com

UK subsidiary office

TEXERE Publishing Limited
71–77 Leadenhall Street
London EC3A 3DE

Tel: +44 (0)20 7204 3644
Fax: +44 (0)20 7208 6701
www.etexere.co.uk

This publication is designed to provide accurate and authoritative information in regard to the subject matter covered. It is sold with the understanding that the publisher is not engaged in rendering legal, accounting, or other professional services. If legal advice or other expert assistance is required, the services or a competent professional person should be sought.

Library of Congress Cataloging in Publication Data has been applied for.

ISBN 1-58799-063-6

Printed in the United States of America

This book is printed on acid-free paper.

10 9 8 7 6 5 4 3 2 1

☠ ☠

WARNING!

☠ ☠

Many of the experiences reported in this book occurred in an earlier millennium.

Corporations make progress.

Things have probably gotten worse.

CONTENTS

THANK YOUS FROM THE THIN AIR

I wish to thank, first of all, the airlines and airports for providing me with such a rich source of materials. It was not easy, I am sure. I wish to thank Betty and Paul for working so creatively to keep my money out of their pockets. I wish to thank Victor Borges for the following line: I wish to thank Mom and Dad for making this possible and Susie and Lisa for making it necessary. (Just kidding, kids. Susie wrote: "If you think Daddy hates flying, you should see him in traffic." And from Lisa: "This is Mintzberg humor at its best. I know. I had to grow up with it.")

I wish to thank Anne an' Ana for sitting next to me on airplanes. After, above and beyond that, I wish to thank Saša for sitting next to me everywhere else. Even on airplanes, Saša makes flying fun.

I wish to thank Joëlle for listening to most of this without always telling me what she really thought. I wish to thank Bill for listening to none of this and always telling me what he really thought (that I should keep my day job). I wish to thank Coralie for trying to tell me what I really thought.

I wish to thank Frances, Harvey, Louis, Kunal, Gordon, Stan, Lee, Joe, and Saša for their noble, though futile efforts to save this book from going over the edge. I wish to thank Mitch, Nancy, and Joe (again) for trying to push this book farther over the edge. I wish to thank McGill University in Montreal and INSEAD near Paris for providing me with day jobs far enough apart to necessitate all that flying. I wish to thank Kate for finding ways to relieve me of my points and, together with Santa, for rendering this manuscript in a form that could be foisted on a suspecting public. (Santa Rodriguez, not Claus, my personal assistant wrote: "Henry hates flying? Ha! He should try it on Christmas eve!")

I wish to thank Hans—boy, do I wish to thank Hans—for keeping this book in the air while it was grounded, until he readied it for takeoff at the London and Frankfurt Book Fairs. Hans believed in Flying as a way to have tons of fun. It would not be here without him. Watch your luggage, Hans.

In London, we met David, Myles, and Martin who were setting up TEXERE. There these guys did something most unusual for publishers these days: They read the book—no, no, let me finish—and then said neither "yes, yes, we believe in you as a way to make tons of money" nor "no, no, and why didn't you include a stamped, self-addressed envelope." They said "Roll up your sleeves, buddy, you've got work to do." And then David rolled up his sleeves and did work too, helping to smooth the edges of an all too sharp manuscript. Thank you, TEXERE guys. You have tons of my respect. If this is how you intend to run your business, then you know nothing about flying.

Almost finally, I wish to thank those valiant workers of the flying business who maintain some semblance of sanity over and above all that insanity on the ground, not to mention having to deal with passengers up here the likes of me.

Finally, high above everyone else, I wish to thank the likes of me, without whom this book could not possibly have been written. Any errors that remain are the fault of the profreader.

> Henry Mintzberg,
> somewhere up in the clouds

WELCOME ABOARD, LADIES AND GENTLEMEN

This is Your Author scribbling. Prior to takeon, while you are settling into your seats to laugh about flying, it is my duty to inform you that this book is about more than flying and therefore no laughing matter.

Nasty rumors have been spreading, by people who read this book carefully, that I have some kind of quarrel with the airlines and the airports. Not true. Some of my best friends spend time in them. I even have the faintest acquaintance of all kinds of nice people who work for them. No, my quarrel is with commercialism, this assumption that we must all be consumed by consumption.

I know that we live in the third millennium, I know that everything is a product and everybody is a market. I know that all human values must be reduced to Shareholder Value. But in hospitals? Churches? Gambling casinos? Ping-pong tournaments? When I discovered that this was happening in the skies, too, so close to the heavens, that was it. I sought my revenge. You are holding it in your hands.

Another rumor, this one circulated by bookmakers and booksellers intent on feeding their children (lavishly), is that you are holding in your hands a book of humor. How can it be when this is a book about Management, or at least about the consequences of Management? Management is a serious business. I know, because down on the ground I write serious books about Management. This book is more so because it flies straight through the abstractions into the everyday reality. It shows what my other books merely say: management may be fine; *Management* is the problem.

Now if you are a manager, you may have trouble understanding this book. No chapter begins: "Five easy steps to. . . ." So I have inserted beneath each chapter title a little cue card that explains its misty connection to Management. If this does not do it—if you insist on finding those easy steps—then may I suggest that you read everything in this book carefully and then do the opposite.

If you are a consumer, you might be tempted to laugh at what follows. Feel free—just so long as you don't do so at the expense of the airlines and airports. For this is not a book about what *they* do to *us.* It is a book about what *we* do to each other.

But please, laugh quietly. The person in the seat next to you is probably a manager, busy arranging your next purchase. Indeed, the person in your own seat may be a manager too, about to arrange my next purchase. But that is only fair, because the person in my seat has already managed to arrange your last purchase.

OK, now fasten your eyes and prepare for this flight of fancy. Bon voyage!

If you want to know why I hate flying,

you will have to wait a minute.

Don't be so impatient.

Just wait here like everyone else.

And can I please see your passport.

Before allowing you to proceed, I am required to ask you some questions:

1. Did you pick this book yourself?
2. Have you left this book unattended at any time since picking it?
3. Does this book contain any substance (?) that could be harmful to its readers?

If you have answered each of the questions—with "Yes," "No," "Maybe," or "Whatever"—we can proceed. Otherwise you must report to Insecurity.

It won't be long now.

Are you starting to get the idea?

Well then, squeeze over

and it will become clearer.

And can I see that passport again.

(You put it in the bottom of your bag, airhead.)

1

FLYING AS A TRANSFORMATIONAL EXPERIENCE

We begin with the chapter about CHANGE. Change must always come first, before anything else, preferably instead of everything else. (Managing change is important; producing goods and services is incidental.) You may have heard—for example, at the beginning of every management speech given during the past thirty years—that we live in times of great change. If so, why do men who give such speeches still wear ties? The fact is that real change—transformation—is rare. Except in airlines, where it happens millions of times every day.

Remember that old saying you probably never heard of, that you can't turn a sow's ear into a silk purse? Maybe it's true. (I never tried.) But let me tell you, airlines are masters at turning cattle into sardines.

If you want to fly somewhere, you must start by being herded—in and out, back and forth, up and down. First, you have to stand in line to get a boarding pass. That is to replace the ticket they just sold you. Then you have to stand in line to *show* your boarding pass. That is to prove you bought the ticket they just took away from you. This lets you stand in line to be checked for bombs. Next, you have to stand in line to give back the boarding pass they just gave you. (If you are flying in Europe, you will probably also have to show your passport here—for the third time.) This done, you get to stand in line to get on the plane, which enables you to stand in line to go down the plane. Eventually, you spot your place in the pen, jammed up against a window. But first you must stand in line one last time while this meathead in front of you takes an interminable time to arrange his trunk overhead. Finally, your way is clear. All you have to do is arrange your own trunk overhead. It won't take but a minute. And now some other bonehead is glaring at you from behind.

At this point, flying becomes a transformational experience. After performing several feats that could land you a job in the circus, you squeeze into your place, utterly transformed: legs locked together, knees tucked up, arms clamped tightly by your sides—because this blubberhead next to you is hogging *your* armrest. (Isn't it supposed to be good fences, rather than single armrests, that make for good neighbors?)

But never mind. You have found your corner of the can. Even if you do feel as if your head and tail have been cut off. Not skinless and boneless, mind you, because this is not a classy place to be. You must never forget that you are in steerage, which the airlines like to call "Economy Class." But if it looks like a sardine and squashes like a sardine, shouldn't we really be calling it Sardine Class?

Now it's the plane's turn to stand in line: first to leave the gate, then to take its place among the dozens of other planes waiting to "take off." Finally, as you clasp your cross, star, or economics book to your breast, this winged can races along the ground like some sort of confused bird trying to hurtle itself into the air. Thus you become airborne, relieved only by the thought that if it worked for Wilbur and Orville Wright, more or less, it will probably work for you.

At this point, I suggest you take a walk. (Ignore those "Seatbelt" signs. They are for people not used to walking downhill.) This will offer a sight like none you will ever see on the face of the earth: every version of the human race—great uncles and grand nieces, trophy and garbage collectors, ostrich breeders and orchestra conductors, pen pals and puddingheads—all preciously lined up in their neat orderly rows. It's enough to make a sardine can look like a disco.

On the ground, when people talk to each other, they stand closer in some cultures, farther in others. Anthropologists like to study this. Except on airplanes. Did you ever meet an anthropologist doing research on an airplane? That is because no culture on earth has ever produced an anthropologist willing to work that close.

2
PROGRAMMING THE PASSENGERS

Here we have a chapter on TRAINING AND DE-
VELOPMENT. This is an expensive business no
longer wasted on employees. They don't stay
around long enough: they insist on getting
downsized. Customers must, however, be
trained to stay around; they must be conditioned to cooperate. McDoughhead's, for example, has been able to replace much of its
cleaning staff with customers, who dutifully
clear the tables. But for the sheer obedience of
their clientele, the airlines are in a class by
themselves.

Once up here, beyond the clouds, our every need is
looked after. Whether we need it or not. Except for
one thing—at least for those of us sitting by the window and tired of the acrobatic routine. This is not really a problem on flights from Buda to Pest. Longer
ones, however, are another matter.

The airlines do provide cute little white bags for those of us going the other way. Trouble is, with one exception I shall get to, so far as I know, no one has used one of those bags since the jet aircraft was introduced in 1952. Some people believe those little white bags provide reassurance. Like the landing gear, I suppose. We'll get to that, too. And then there are those who use these bags to save money on stationery.

Everything else up here takes place on cue. Somebody is pressing the buttons down at head office. As the plane leaves the gate, a flight attendant at the front of the cabin performs some kind of ritualistic dance on cue, which everyone else ignores on cue. This is accompanied by an announcement in a strange language known only to the airline people:

"WelcomeaboardthisAirBlaBlaflightfromBudatoPestwithstopsinPuneandPerth. . . ."

This greeting apparently comes in different languages, because recently, after going through something similar in a Montreal departure lounge, the airline person looked up and asked, "Did I just do that in French?" Everyone shrugged.

Then the drinks come by, on cue. Three pieces of ice are dropped into each cup, on cue, cue, cue. "Can I have the can?" you can ask. Later, a tray drops before you, on cue. Something they claim to be food is placed upon it, and you nevertheless eat it, on cue.

Programming the Passengers

Some time after this, on cue, the lights dim and the *Entertainment* appears, on a little screen on the horizon. This is yours to enjoy through the head of the basketball player sitting in front of you. The sound is beamed to you, more or less on cue, through earphones designed especially for the airlines in 1903 by Alexander Graham Bell. First are *The Exercises,* to relieve the tension. Bending fingers. Knotting stomachs. Opening nostrils (in search of air). Stretching imaginations (by pretending to flap arms). During the movie that follows, everyone laughs repeatedly, precisely on cue, without uttering a sound. We are quite the sight, we hundreds of human sardines sitting there and responding like Skinner pigeons.

Finally, the movie ends, with assurances that everyone will live happily ever after. That is the cue for all the aisle people and the acrobats to leap up and line up at the loo. This can of cans has been empty for three hours.

One thing in all of this must happen off cue (although just as it's your turn at the loo). If the airplane encounters the slightest breeze, "Your Captain" is obliged to say: "This is Your Captain screaming," followed by: "We are passing through a zone of turbulence. Would you kindly return to your seats, fasten your seatbelts, and put your seatbacks to their most uncomfortable position." It is at this point that 375 clicks follow in perfect unison, on cue. You have just experienced *The Airline Salute.*

3

GETTING LOOPED

We come now to CUSTOMER SERVICE. Customer Service is when they smile at you in the front office while trying to squeeze more money out of you in the back office.

Ahhh, you say, why put up with all this herding and squeezing? Someone else is probably paying, so why not go Business Class. Be a zillionaire sardine.

Did you ever open one of those fancy cans? Do you really believe a sardine feels better just because it's going at several times the price? They may look elegant, all those little fish sitting there in their olive oil. But please be assured they are no happier.

In fact, Business Class is a confusing label. Thanks partly to the heroic efforts of the airlines themselves, Business Class has become more than just a place in an airplane. So once again, let's call it as it quacks: Pampered Class. The objective is to treat you disgustingly well. This must be to alleviate their guilt. They refer to this as *Customer Service.* I long for customer service.

At this point, I must make one thing perfectly clear. Flying for me is damage control. Like buying gasoline; worse still, like refilling the stapler. No joy; just get it over with as quickly and as painlessly as possible. I don't need any service attendant smiling at me, or some face on the tube telling me how much they love me and my money. All I want to do in an airplane is vegetate, which, for me, means to read, uninterrupted. You may prefer to sleep. Same thing.

"Excuse me, sir, your Alexander Graham Bell earphones." . . . "Pardon me, sir, we have these duty-free gold-plated gumdrops." . . . "Sir, your very own teddy bear."*

Now they have a new twist. Computers have *Personalized* the service. Subliminal cue cards have been submerged electronically in the brains of the flight attendants. "Excuse me, Mr. Mintzberg, your Chateau Chirac 1943," . . . "More Velveeta, Mr. Mintzberg?" . . . "Your coloring book, Mr. Mintzberg." Peace and quiet, Mr. Mintzberg? No, never peace and quiet for Mr. Mintzberg. They are Mistermintzberging me to death. One day I am going to register as Mr. Jackass.

---

* Because you may already be getting the impression that I am inclined to exaggerate slightly, let me just say that I exaggerate least when I seem to do so the most. Stories about flying require no exaggeration. Blimey Airways used to run an ad campaign showing an adult's head over a child's body, tucked into one of their gargantuan seats, with a teddy bear by its side. That is you and me, in the mind of some marketing executive.

Getting Looped

Why don't they just leave me alone? I once asked this profound question of an Air Kanuk flight attendant sitting next to me, "deadheading" home. She was quite polite about it, although she refused to give back *my* armrest. "But we are told to do this," she pleaded. "It's called 'looping.'"

Looping! They have a name for it. I've been looped all these years. I'll bet I could sue them for breach of privacy. There must be freedom from expression somewhere off this world.

Think about it. Fully grown adult human beings are sitting in offices and being paid to arrange such things. First a drink. Headphones next. Then the nuts; don't forget the nuts. The real drinks follow. More nuts. Then the menu (nuts). . . . And *they* refer to these poor flight attendants' simply trying to get home as *deadheading.*

I asked Louis about looping. Louis is a marketing professor at our place who used to work for Air Kanuk. "But the passengers *like* looping," Louis lamented. "They have all kinds of Marketing Research to prove it." (We'll get to *Marketing Research* too.)

But how much looping do they like, Louis? I mean, is this like happiness—insatiable? Where does looping end and pestering begin?

More to the point, when does Managing end and thinking begin? This kind of stuff may be great for the maintenance department. They have engines in there—

delicate creatures in need of the gentlest of care. But up here, in the sky, unbeknownst to them, we are real people. Hey, gang, we live and breathe up here. Or, at least, we try to. Give us a break.

Look, I have an idea: Treat me like cargo. Isn't that why you have Marketing—to *think* of me like cargo? So why can't you treat me like cargo? You know, just get me from A to B without damage. Why can't we passengers get that kind of respect?

There is this joke about a guy who says to his wife: "If you don't leave me alone, I'll find someone else who will." Take heed, airlines.

4

FULLY FLEECED

*This chapter demonstrates the use of TECHNIQUE—
in pricing and partnering. The object is objectivity;
the subject is humanity. A Technique is something
that can be used in place of a brain. Techniques
are very popular in Management.*

Why go Pampered Class? If not for the looping, then what for? The food, you say? We'll bring that up soon enough. The status? Just because Virginal Airways calls it "Upper Class" and Air Kanuk's label is "Executive First"? The space—the fact that the armrests are several meters wide? You think that ensures a good night's sleep? (We'll get to that too.) Or avoids the acrobatic routine? By the time the guy in front of you has dropped his seat back 196° and the gal next to you has positioned her television set at 87°, all you can do is lie back and dream about the wonders of Sardine Class (where the seats go back $1\frac{3}{8}$°).

In the meantime, the burning question: How much does this particular "good night's sleep" really cost?

Not much, in fact. Have you ever noticed that a Pampered Class ticket costs only $1.75 more than one in Sardine Class? Well, OK, I'm really referring to what they call "Full-Fare Economy," which should really be called Full-Fleece Economy. Alice says that it serves as the perfect introduction to the wonderland of airline pricing.

Full-Fleece Economy is a fare that has been especially developed for people who have suddenly lost a distant relative. Who else would buy it? If you stay over a Saturday night or fly at 4:00 A.M. or are chummy with a travel agent or promise to sit still—in other words, if you do almost anything conceivable except claim that your family pit bull died yesterday—you get a discount.*

And I mean a discount! Good thing that poor guy without the pit bull is too upset to speak to his neighbors. He might discover that he paid more than they did. I mean more than *all* of them—across the entire row. Here he sits fighting over an armrest with his travel agent's niece, whose ticket was purchased with the commission earned on his. She could have gone to the movies in Peoria. Instead, she decided to visit Paris.

---

* Some airlines do give discounts to those who have lost distant relatives. But only if they are distant only in distance. And many do not tell the passengers, before they leave, how much they are saving. More anxiety; this "Compassionate Refund" comes later. It can range from almost nothing to just over 50 percent, which brings the price down from Absurd to Outrageous. So be careful who dies, and where.

Fully Fleeced

Lest you think that I could be exaggerating, let me quote some real figures. They prove, beyond any doubt, that I am exaggerating far less than the airlines themselves.

Montreal to Paris, round trip, Air Kanuk (in $U.S.):

Pampered Class	$3,256
Full-Fleece Economy	2,654
Cheapest Sardine Class	572
(Charters are cheaper)	

Same plane, same route, same air (but less of it); almost six times the price in Pampered Class, even if you do arrive several seconds earlier. (Sales are superior. Uncle Sam Airways, for example, could get you from Boston to Buffalo and back for $709, Full-Fleece Economy, or, on sale in July 2000, for $98. The charge was a tad more to get you from Philadelphia to Frankfurt and back—$3,792, Full-Fleece Economy. Unless you preferred the sale in January 2001: $245. Cheaper by the dozen.)

OK, so the food in Pampered Class is better. Not good, just better. But do you need that food in any class? I can fly from Prague to London and back for $757, Full-Fleece Economy, big-shot airline. Or I can fly from Prague to London and back, No-Fleece Economy, small-shot airline, no sale, no food, for $127. Two lunches—those lunches!—plus some peanuts, for $630. You decide.

So what's a guy without a pit bull to do? Easy: Stay home. For the same expenditure, he can have more time with his bereaved family: 126 hours, 22 minutes, and 51.4 seconds, to be exact. On the telephone. And he gets to stretch out his legs in the bargain.

Now you begin to get an idea of what that good night's sleep really costs. Rather pricey, if you can sit still. But what's the point of belonging to the world's newest class if you can't get a couple of hours of sleep for a few thousand bucks?

We are not through yet. Get this: If you spend your spare time reading the speeches of airline executives, you will have discovered that this is the age of competition: fierce competition, turbulent markets, the horrors of deregulation. How can the airlines possibly cope?

Easy. As a kid, did you ever go to summer camp? Take a swim in the lake? Remember how, when they blew the whistle, everyone had to find their buddy and hold up hands to prove they didn't drown? Well, the airlines have been doing much the same thing in recent years. Except that when these guys hold up hands with their buddies, it means they are probably swimming in black ink, not drowning in red.

In the flying business, buddies are called "Partners." When the partners stand in a great big circle and hold up their hands all around the globe, it's called an "Alliance." An Alliance is like a gang—a set of "best friends" who hang out together. These gangs roam the skies, not the streets: The members share reservation systems, they go shopping together for engines, combine points, lose luggage—that sort of thing. Keeps the globe safe for the big guys.

Sometimes they even share airplanes, and passengers. You never know whose plane you'll find yourself on (or off, if you read your ticket correctly and went to the wrong terminal). You're booked on Air Feather but you find yourself flying on Air Lead. "But the ads say that Air Feather has a light touch," you protest. "I don't need the solid friendship promised by Air Lead. I took a marketing course once. They told me that branding is important. So I read every ad religiously, and then select my suppliers with the utmost of care."

"Can I see your passport?" they reply.

Look, if this is all these guys think of their brands, what are we supposed to think of them? More importantly, what do they think of us when they shift us from one airline to another?

Let's say I'm taking a little trip to Tierra del Fuego and I'm a worrier. I have a choice between Air Bang and Air Breeze. I check very carefully and discover that Air Breeze has a better safety record. So I book my ticket on Air Breeze. They don't bother to tell my ticket or me that they have put me on Air Bang. The plane blows a tire upon landing, and we slip off the runway. I fracture my left pinkie. Upon sliding down the chute, I discover that I have been on Air Bang all along. Imagine the fun lawyers could have with this one.

Now if you have been following the prices lately, you will have noticed another interesting thing. They have been racing downward. Yes. This is the result of that fierce competition you have been reading about. Every airline *does* have one dastardly competitor against which it competes viciously: itself.

Here we have "Yield Management," one of those *Techniques* that can be used in place of brains. Techniques are designed by webheads.

Think of Yield Management as high-tech scalping, except that the objective is for the airlines to scalp themselves. They have to fill every single seat—at any price.

As soon as an empty seat comes up, the hawking begins. No seat must go unfilled. When the airplane finally takes off, 479 seats may well be going at 479 different prices, from $4.79 to $47,900. I heard a story about a kid who was delivering flowers to a gate agent in Idaho. He used his tip to go to India.

But all this is small potatoes. If these guys really want to fix up their poor old bottom lines, I have an idea that will save them billions. Maybe they'll pass a few pennies of it on to us. A modest illustration will explain.

Fully Fleeced

The other day, I booked a seat at the opera. I called after the performance. "I booked a seat at the ballet too," I said. "I didn't feel like going to the opera." "No problem," they replied, "Please feel free to do this again. We appreciate your money and especially not having to clean up your popcorn."

"Hey, wait a minute," I cried. "You keep my money? You people don't even give miles."

Same problem when I book a hotel room. They actually expect me to show up. I can't even get away with this on the train. So why do airlines let me book to my heart's content, at least Full-Fleece and above, without having to buy a ticket or even show up?

Simple: It's all for me. Another form of *Customer Service.* If I need to fly to Come by Chance, Newfoundland, I can book nine seats on each of eight airlines at seven different times. Take my choice.

Except for a few incidental details. I can't get half the reservations I won't honor because everyone else is doing the same thing. Indeed, the reason I have to book so many seats is because everyone else is booking so many seats. Then there's the overbooking, followed by the bumping. The more the airlines bump, the more we passengers have to book. The circle is vicious indeed. You see, we fleece ourselves, we poor passengers.

I really want to go on Flighty Airways' midnight express. But it's fully booked. I can't risk it, even though I know it will fly half empty. So I have settled for Air Chance at noon, and have rescheduled my meeting. Let's see, that meeting will probably end about 9:15, and it's a 15-minute ride to the airport, so, with all the herding, I should be OK for the 12 o'clock. I'd better make a backup booking or two: on the 12:15 and the 12:30 flights. Also the 12:45, just in case. But I have to be careful. These guys might have computers. They could cross-check and then cancel all my reservations. Computers are smart; I must be even smarter. I know, I'll book the 12:00 as Mr. Jackass, the 12:15 as Mr. Jakass, the 12:30 as Mr. Jackas, and the 12:45 as Mr. Jerkass. If they don't believe it's me, I can always claim their donkey on the phone spelt my name wrong.

Long lines. I make it to the gate at 12:28. Mustn't miss the 12:30, or else I will have to wait for the 12:45. No problem, they say. The 12:30 flight is not going to leave before 2:30. A little rearranging to be done. Overbooking, you know.

"Calm down, everybody," I hear. "This is an airport, a proper place. You are all waiting to fly—maybe. Why on earth would you be so anxious? Now, many of you will have to wait for the next available flight—on Friday. As for the lucky few with boarding cards, we are offering, as compensation for flying next week, a complimentary excursion to the ice floes, where you can pet the poor seals. In Newfoundland, passengers and seals understand each other. We have dozens of members of our staff here for no other purpose than to sort all this out."

I amble up to the agents. "My name is Mr. Jackass," I bray haughtily. "I fly a lot." "Yes, we know," they reply, "we hear you are writing a book about flying, Mr. Jackas [they pronounce it Jack-*az*]. We have rebooked you next month. In return, you get a free trip to Harbour Harbour, Newfoundland. One week long. No substitutions. Unless you'd prefer two weeks in Toronto." (Their computer knows I'm from Montreal.)

"This is outrageous," I say. "You can see my bona fide booking right there on your screen. Why, your donkey of an agent has even misspeld my name. How can you have the nerve to give *my* seat—*my very own seat*—to some stranger? And while we're at it, let me tell you, your prices are outrageous. Just look at all your people hanging around negotiating changes. All because *you* overbooked. If *you* kept *my* seat for *me*, *you* wouldn't need all these people, and think of all the money *we* would save. Next time I go to Newfoundland, I shall take the train. Better still, I will stay home and go to the opera. *Those* people never give away *my* seat. Take that!"

You should have seen the agents quiver. Not just because I am so terrifying. Those agents quiver from the day they take that job. They never stop quivering until they are carried out to the hospitals and asylums while another set of agents is being led in. But Air Chance doesn't care. Back at Headquarters, it's all perfectly calm. No overbooking in the boardroom; a seat there for everyone.

Now how on earth (I hope you are asking yourself) could those smart people who run the airlines have gotten themselves into such a mess: multiple reservations, overbooked flights, empty reserved seats, delayed planes, extra gate staff, anxious passengers, last-minute negotiations, free compensation trips, terrifying Jackasses, quivering agents, and nervous breakdowns, not to mention trashed boarding cards? I will let you figure that one out for yourself. (Hint: Read Chapters 1–3, 4, 5–11, 14, and 15.) But there is a solution: Replace all those financial wizards who run the airlines with people who have managed real companies: Operas.

5
POINTS PAYOLA

This chapter is about solidifying CUSTOMER LOYALTY. You must first know who your Customers are—not those who pay, but those who get others to pay. Then you must instill Loyalty in these people, which is tricky when you have just trashed your brand. But if you think back to Christmastime and that bottle of whiskey. . . .

We're not done with pricing just yet. Don't forget the points—the "miles." No problem; the airlines never let you forget them. No sooner do you get off one plane than they're looping you in the mails about how to get you on another. You'd think they'd be smart enough to keep quiet. Or at least offer you a ride on a train.

But no. Barbara wrote to me recently. "Dear Dr. Mintzberg," she started sweetly. "We're a bit puzzled. On one hand, we know that you enjoy the comforts and high level of personal service you receive when flying [Blimey] Airways. [Read the book Barbara.] On the other hand, we can't figure out why you're not flying

[Blimey] Airways across the Atlantic." Think of it this way, Barbara: I haven't been going to London lately. I refuse to fly to Paris via London just for the sake of your British food.

But I don't think Barbara understood, because she offered me—yes, me—**"Double miles on [Blimey] Airways—across the Atlantic and all over the world!"** (This is Barbara's **bold face.**) Wowee! "It's almost beyond belief!" the very expensive accompanying card said. Almost.

But maybe Barbara did understand, because when she claimed to "look forward to seeing [me] on board soon," I took the bait. I raced out to get those **double miles** to London, and then on to Paris. But where was Barbara? I was stuck with that British food and no Barbara in sight.

Now, let's take a good look at this points business. Whenever anyone tries to bribe you with your own money, watch out. It's a sure sign that you're being overcharged. After all, someone has to be paying for all those fancy brochures, all the Barbaras with their **bold faces,** all the people not answering the phones—not to mention a mite left over for the line at the bottom. If they really wanted to give back your money, wouldn't they simply write you a check and be done with it?

Something else must be going on here. Now to those of you who fly on business, and are so very sensitive, this is going to come as a terrible shock. Please, brace yourself. *They are not bribing you with your own money at all.* There, I said it.

Today, we call it points. In an earlier incarnation, it was called "payola." Now, it is business as usual. Back then, it was scandal. Payola was the label pegged on radio disk jockeys who took money from recording companies in exchange for playing their releases. Imagine that: One party taking a reward from a second party for spending a third party's money. Like accepting a bottle of whiskey from a supplier at Christmas. Or a few dollars from an interest group to run an election campaign. Unthinkable.

So unthinkable, in fact, that even the tax collectors— hardly slouches when it comes to the laying on of hands—are afraid to touch this one. Is it because they fly too? Or because you just don't mess with the Business Class?

But wait a minute. "It's not like that," I am told by legions of people who have been well rehearsed on this issue. They have concocted a wonderful explanation for points payola. It goes like this: It is such a hardship to fly, so disagreeable to be away from the family you hardly know, so stressful to be frolicking in France rather than doing the dishes in Des Moines, that points are the least you deserve.

Now beats me where anyone gets this idea that flying isn't fun. Even so, would not this world be a better place if these poor travelers were properly compensated by their employers instead of being bribed by their suppliers? That way, they could at least trade up their BMWs for proper Lamborghinis. Maybe even find a cheaper flight on another airline now and again.

While personally waiting to be so purified, I have accumulated zillions of points, as you might imagine. But they have not corrupted me, simply because I never get around to using them. I am too busy flying—on other people's money.

I did try once, years ago. I asked Air Gaul for a tiny little upgrade on a flight to India. Bombay is a long way from Paris, and because I was staying over a month of Saturdays, could book decades in advance, am chummy with my travel agent, and usually sit still, I got a really good deal in Sardine Class. I could hardly have found a taxi to Versailles at a cheaper price. Finally, I could use some of those points to sit where, by then, I should have become accustomed to sitting. So I called Air Gaul.

Calling Air Gaul is almost a chapter unto itself (coming next). Eventually, I reached a Mme. Ratched. She's the sister of that nurse in *One Flew Over the Cuckoo's Nest.* I told her about going to India, and about sitting where I should have become accustomed. "That will cost you 50,000 miles," she said, adding, I am sure with a smirk on her face, while I crumbled in despair: "One way." Yes, 50,000 miles was what they wanted back then just for a few hours in their Pampered Class. Think of it this way: I had to fly eighty million meters in order

to walk eight meters forward in one of their cabins.*
Needless to say, I kept all my points. But for what reason, I cannot say.

Actually I can. Kate, my personal assistant until she
flew into public relations, used my points with great
glee. She didn't mind the restrictions, like having to fly
on Friday the 13ths. Kate once flew from Montreal to
Bangor, Maine, via Detroit, then Boston, and finally
Portland (actually Maine, not Oregon). It took her eight
hours. Kate could not have walked that fast.

As I cumulated all these points, I advanced in the
Great Airlines Image Sweepstakes. I used to be Tin on
one airline. As I flew, I moved up—to Bronze, Silver,
Gold, and, finally, Diamond. When I graduated from
Gold to Diamond, a military band was dispatched to my
office to play "Diamond Is a Passenger's Best Friend,"
while a salivating vice president handed me a diamond-
plated certificate. The next year, when I made a trip or
two less, I was required to take a bus to the airline headquarters, climb the back stairs, and hand my diamond-
plated certificate back to the nearest cleaning person.

Those were the good old days. Modest. We have
moved on since then. In the ever escalating war of
woolly words, we now have Prestige and Elite, Celebrity

---

* I say meters, but Air Gaul gives "miles," not kilometers, even if the
word does break your tongue in French. Napoleon may have made
the country metric 200 years ago, but kilometers are smaller than
miles, and the bottom line is, after all, the bottom line.

and Chosen, Fat Cat and Top Dog, even Chairman's Preferred (I'll bet!). As the categories have become finer and
the exaggerations coarser, the marketing people have
had to scour all twenty volumes of *The Oxford English
Dictionary* for words that have yet to be contaminated.
Accordingly, I recently received the following letter:

Dear Mr. Jackass:

You will be enthralled to discover that your latest
flight from Buda to Pest has elevated you from
Majesty to Maharajah. This gives you the privilege of skipping customs and immigration altogether, as well as riding into each flight on top of
a properly adorned elephant. Please be assured
that the elephant will be installed in the seat
next to you—we have asked it to be as polite as
possible and have given it an especially large little white bag—so that you can mount right up
there to ride off the flight in the manner to which
you became accustomed riding on. Should you
add another eighty million millimeters to your
record, that will put you in the Pharaoh category,
which enables you to remain in your living room,
properly encased, while we bring wherever you
wish to go directly to you.

Glowingly,

Air Image

WE INTERRUPT THIS DIATRIBE TO BRING YOU

ANA

A SHORT STORY ABOUT WHY I LOVE FLYING

Two shoes in sight. One black, shiny. The other brown, scruffy. No sock visible above the black shoe. A white sock above the scruffy one—well, slightly gray really; washed too many times. Beyond this, black leather pants, maybe a little too chic, stretched out next to old, frayed jeans. Nothing else to report, short of stealing a sideways glance.

A sideways glance. Not to establish gender. That has already been done by all concerned (him, and you hopefully; not her).

She reads a book, in Spanish, highlighting like mad. What in Spanish can possibly be so interesting? He scribbles madly, a story about sighting two shoes. ¡Now that's interesting! Still no face clearly in sight. Still the intrigue, though.

Takeoff. More sideways glances. She puts a fancy metal clip on her page and closes the book. He tried one of those decades ago—she was probably not yet even in diapers—but the page always tore. Then she rolls the other way and goes to sleep. Ah, tired, probably depressed. Or maybe just stayed up to watch some dumb late-night movie.

He puts down his pen—or at least intends to after finishing this sentence—to fetch his bag, there to find some proper paper. Better than having to write this on the back of another story.

Done. Maneuvered forth and back. From that angle, a sock has been revealed. Sheer, gray. Could that mean it was not a late-night movie after all? He has stepped delicately over the outstretched pants, the shiny shoes, the sheer socks. All in Row 1. Come to think of it, why is she flying business class from Toronto to Montreal? He, after all, has an excuse. Just came in from Tokyo, business class. So they put him here. Ah so, maybe she has come in from Rio. Anything but Toronto.

He would have preferred to bump that shoe. "Oh, I am ever so sorry. Do you come from Rio? What in Spanish [OK, Portuguese] could possibly be so interesting? I'm writing a story about us." But no, he's too polite. Well, let's just call it that. Anyway, he doesn't want to find out it was that late-night movie after all.

Things are happening now. A trolley goes by, oblivious to the drama unfolding here. He asks for water. They each get a little bowl of mixed nuts. He digs in. You already know about his resistance to temptation, at least when it can't talk back. So while he feasts, worrying about gaining weight, she sleeps, worrying about.... But that is the very point: What does she worry about? Is it worth his worrying about? Can it possibly be as important as his gaining weight? All he currently knows for certain is that she doesn't know what she's missing in that little bowl.

Now what?

She stirs, that's what. Problems in Rio? Back to sleep. But no, she's up. Tries a nut. Yawns. Another nut. Apparently can't resist temptation either. Asks for water, in what sounds like normal English. So much for Rio. Probably Hamilton.

They drink their respective water. A big diamond appears on her little finger. Not entirely his kind of woman. Come to think of it, the leather pants don't really go with the English.

He is just about to burst into conversation, finally ("You from Montreal?" so clever), when she picks up the airline magazine. Can't interrupt her now. But wait, Hamiltonians don't usually read Spanish, let alone Portuguese. They probably read airline magazines.

She puts it down. Better do something—the airplane is in descent. "Been cold a long time here?" he asks. (Now that's clever.)

He gets a groggy, "Excuse me?" Then the profundity of it sinks in. "Sorry, I don't know; I'm not from here." The English is accented.

"Where are you from?"

"Brazil," she says. No kidding. She just said Brazil!

Now he's allowed to look. Rather pretty, an interesting face. A clean, direct look. Doesn't go with the pants. Not in this hemisphere, at least. Older than thought at first, second, third glance. Was probably in diapers after all.

He can't leave well enough alone: "Rio?"

"No, Brasilia," she says. Serves him right. He nonethe-
less

recovers.

"Is it as bad a place as they say?"

"No, not at all." She likes Brasilia.

Now they're flying. She was raised in Brasilia, one of
the few. He asks why she has come here, what she does.
Must always ask that damnable question. But this
time the answer takes a funny form: "I follow my presi-
dent around." "Oh." Then the possible triviality of it
sinks in: not another MBA? No sooner has he left his
world of management education than there appears
yet another MBA.

But no, this time he's saved. Her President runs
Brazil. She's a reporter for a big Brazilian television
network. Her President is coming to Canada, so, so
is she.

The snow on the ground surprises her. Him too, ac-
tually. Late April, up in this hemisphere, it should be
spring. But the weather always does provide thirty
million Canadians with something to talk about.

Soon she admits to escaping Brasilia for Rio or São Paulo every weekend. She loves Rio, she says. Just as he suspected all along: deep in their souls, that vital connection. He once spent three hours in Rio, touring in a taxi between flights. He loved it too. Most unusual coincidence. Fate.

She's tired. Long trip. He tells her he's writing a book called Why I Hate Flying. She says she reads in airplanes. He already knows that. Then she notices him scribbling madly.

"Are you writing a book?" she asks.

"No," he answers, "I'm writing a story."

Now here the conversation could have taken a serious turn: "Why must you write this now? Are you rude, disinterested, or just plain weird?" Then he would have had to say: "No, not entirely all of the above. I have no memory. If I don't get the conversation down immediately, I forget it. Could I ask you to speak a little more slowly, please." But no, she doesn't ask.

A flight attendant appears, bending down. Things are taking a serious turn after all. Apparently the shiny shoes were meant to grace the streets of Ottawa. That, after all, is where Presidents go. They ended up next to the scruffy ones by mistake. Plans are being hatched to get them to Ottawa.

"Montreal is a lot nicer place than Ottawa," he admits, maintaining the honesty of their relationship. He resists the temptation to add that it is sort of like Rio compared with Brasilia—and this, after all, is a weekend. Her President is not coming for a day or two, she admits, but still she wants to get to Ottawa.

Just as he always knew: no charm. Or is it no luck? Better still: no time. He should have interrupted that airline magazine after all. "Anyway, if you change your mind and want a lift to the city, let me know. My daughter is picking me up at the airport." See: such a nice family man.

Landing. That damnable flight attendant again: "We're gong to get you off the plane first." So, with a "Nice to meet you," she's gone. Just like that.

He passes the transit counter. She is deep in negotiation. He waits for his luggage, deep in mindlessness. Daughter arrives, claiming to be freshly in love.

Then she appears again, freshly rebooked. A brief word, a warm touch on his arm, and off she goes to find her bags. They wait respectively. Then he gets an idea(!). Writes his home number on a business card. His bags arrive, same time as hers. He hands her the card as he leaves: "If you run into any problem, give me a call." Especially if you don't. She takes it, smiles pleasantly, and heads for the gate. Then, for no apparent reason, she turns around and calls back: "My name is Ana."

6

FLYING BY PHONE

Now we come to the chapter on EFFICIENCY. Efficiency is very important. Without It, there would be no organizations. With it, there are fewer organizations. That is because efficiency experts are happiest when there are no costs, even if that means there are no customers.

Back to that time I called Air Gaul about the miles. Calling the airlines can make flying seem like a breeze.

I did eventually get a human voice—after almost ten minutes. Well, sort of a human voice. The woman was not terribly interested in how long I had been waiting—it had been like this for four weeks, she said, as if that made it proper. Just then, I heard a beep on my phone. "Could you hold for just a moment, please?" I asked politely, "I have another call." "No," she said, and hung up.

So I wrote to Air Gaul. Their computer answered immediately. I was assured that "a great deal of planning goes into the staffing." They "sincerely hope[d] that [they] may be privileged to serve me again and have a chance to prove that this experience was an exception." Four weeks of exception.

It would have been callous of me to ignore such a nice offer, so I called back some time later. I was sick in bed at the time, with not much else to do. Why not call Air Gaul's points people so that I could write back and say, "You were right—I waited only four milliseconds." Not quite. I got music, alternating with reassuring messages about how much they appreciate my business. One voice even said, "We are particularly busy at the moment." Finally, another voice, at the 11-minute mark, no kidding. "Please call back later," it said, and hung up, without so much as a chirpy little "Ciao!"

A glutton for punishment, I tried again a couple of years later, from San Diego. New time, new place, even a new message. But the same Air Gaul. "Your patience is very much appreciated," the voice said—30 times. (I counted.)

Things had improved, however, because I finally did get a real voice—at the 21-minute mark. (The things I do for research.) She was actually very nice. Almost worth the wait. The volume had been especially high, she explained, and "A bunch of people are coming in from training next week." Phew. Thank goodness I called this week.

Corporations, you may recall, make progress. Come the new millennium and I am still trying to reach Air Gaul. This time it is about a bag of mine that has gone missing between Montreal and Prague, via Paris. The Air Gaul office in Prague cannot get any information, so I ask for the number in Paris. It answers immediately. The voice says that if I would like to report a lost bag, I should write Air Gaul a letter. It gives an address and hangs up. It does not add: "While waiting for your bag, we suggest you eat cake."

Now that we are on—really off—bags, let me take you to North America, during the first summer of the new millennium, kind of a repeat of 476 A.D., when the Huns, Vandals, and Goths were overrunning the Roman Empire. Anyone who loved flying before was fully cured in this Summer of 00.

Air Kanuk, having just gobbled up its arch rival, has become a near-monopoly in most of its northland. The shareholders are delighted—at least those who don't have to fly Air Kanuk.

I *do* have to fly Air Kanuk. And I don't own shares (as you might have guessed).

OK, so my bag didn't make it from Frankfurt to Montreal. These things happen. I fill out the form and go home. Trouble is, I have to fly to Toronto tomorrow, and I need something in that bag, but not that bag itself, not to Toronto and back. So I call Air Kanuk. I give up after 20 minutes, and take the advice of The Voice, which suggests that I call back before 9:00 A.M., when things are quieter. Duly jet-lagged, I call at 6:00 A.M. The Voice was right. I get a guy—after 30 minutes. "No problem," he says, "I'll mark your bag 'hold'; you come to the luggage door at the airport before your flight, pick up the phone there, and punch the Air Kanuk key. We'll come right out with your bag, you take what you need, and then we'll send it where you tell us." So simple.

I stand outside the door and punch Air Kanuk. One happy finger. One miserable me: ten minutes and no answer. A guy walks by and laughs: "Still not answering?" he says. "I gave up after ten minutes." So I do too. Better today's plane than not yesterday's luggage.

In Toronto, in between meetings, I call Santa (not Claus, Rodrigues, my assistant). She answers immediately. (If you have any questions about this book, do not call Santa. She will keep you on hold for months.)

"Save me," I plead.

"What is it this time?" she queries. I tell her about my bag being on hold (not to mention the phone). Can she extract it and have a courier deliver what I need to Toronto?

Later, Santa calls back. She has given up after being held on hold for an hour and a half. (At this moment, I begin to develop an appreciation for Air Gaul.) Call the Big Cheese, I suggest. She does. His assistant (who must be named Claus) gets us the bag real quick. (Does she know about *Why I Hate Flying?*)

Flying by Phone

The Big Cheese is actually aware of these problems—maybe because his airline is being featured on the media, day after day, horror story upon horror story. Mine is minor. In this summer of the passengers' discontent, Air Kanuk is loaded with all sorts of other baggage. Like a plane that came in from China (reported in the *Globe and Mail,* August 5) with sixteen happy families aboard, each with a newly adopted baby girl—a bunch of very small, very tired, and probably very traumatized baby girls who may not have entirely appreciated the novelty of flying. Seventeen hours *en route.* And then, in Toronto, four more hours *en tarmac* before someone managed to get them to a gate. So sorry, they were told upon disembarking at 2:00 A.M., the baggage staff has gone home. Report tomorrow to pick up your clean diapers, etc. (Stand outside that door, mommies and daddies, and pound Air Kanuk.)

Now don't get me wrong. The company had a problem, so its president sprang into action—immediately. He called in the PR brigade. So here he was, on the media, day after day, promise upon promise. "Our 180-day commitment," he kept telling us. Air Kanuk will solve its problems in 180 days. "You've got my word on it," he said. Gee, thanks, Mr. President. What's the rush? A few hours to get out the ads, and half a year to fix the problems? We're waiting for our luggage and he's *Managing the Merger.* "Hang on, ye without bags," he was saying, "Air Kanuk is going to answer the phones in February." Just when Canada will be dozing under a blanket of soft snow. Air Kanuk could probably fire half its staff and still do better in February. Come to think of it, Air Kanuk could fire all its entire telephone staff and hardly do much worse. Here we have a company that is *efficient*.

It's all the rage these days for heroic chief executives to clamber aboard the tube and tell us how they are fixing things. Maybe they should sit quietly in the background and stop breaking things. Even let the passengers fix a thing or two. Me, for instance. *Why I Hate Flying* is due out in February too. You've got my word on it. Better still, you've got my book! No need to call Santa.

Now, why must there be any problem these days with phones. They can, after all, be connected to computers. Computers are smart; they have even learned how to speak. How I yearn for those hour-and-a-half holds:

Thank you for calling Air Wait. Please settle into a very soft chair with a very long drink.

[P-A-U-S-E]

- For service in Latin, touch V.
- For service in English, touch £.

[P-A-U-S-E]

- If you are calling about a ticket on which your name has been spelled incorrectly, please touch S-P-E-L-D-B-A-D.

- If you are calling about having to wait interminably for this line, please hold.

[Much later]

- Thank you for holding. That is kind of you. We hope you appreciate that our time is so much more valuable than yours. While you are waiting for us, you will be delighted to listen to our advertisements instead of your thoughts.

[A-D-V-E-R-T-I-S-E-M-E-N-T-S]

- If you wish to speak to our leader, touch *.

- If you are calling about our prices, pound on the # key.

- If you wish to register a complaint, punch !$&@%.

[P-A-U-S-E]

- If, in spite of all this, you still wish to leave a message, then please speak after the beep.

[L-O-N-G P-A-U-S-E]

- Please do not speak until you hear the beep. After leaving your message, please touch B-Y or just hang up.

[P-A-U-S-E]

- "Beep. Beep. Beep. Beep. Beep. Beep. Beep. Beep. Beep. Beep. Beep. Beep.

[L-O-N-G P-A-U-S-E]

- Beeeeeeeeeeeeeeeeeeeeeeeeeeeeeeeeeeeeeeeeeeeeeep.
- "Hello, Air Wait? I am sorry to bother you but. . . ."
- Beep. Click.

Now, if you are lucky enough to know the name of a real person in the airline, you can skip all this—well, sort of. Instead, you can go directly to the following:

- Hello!! This is Paraphernalia Philidendrum in the Customer Salvage Department. I cannot answer the phone right now, or ever for that matter, but if you leave your name, number, and size of bank account, I will get back to you just as soon as I feel like it.

There follows a long pause and then a voice from a mouth shaped like a keyboard. (The sequence that follows is real, as real as the times I waited for Air Gaul and Air Kanuk. I had to call back three times to get it all down.*)

---

* OK, so it was Bruce's line, and he works for a business school. But Bruce flies a lot.

Flying by Phone

- To disconnect, press 1. [Can't I just hang up?]

- To enter another number, press 2. [What if the other number I want to enter is not 2?]

- If you still wish to leave a message for this person, press 3 [P-A-U-S-E] or simply stay on the line. [Oh! I never would have thought of that.]

- If you need assistance, press 0. [Are you kidding?]

- At the tone, please leave your message. [Paraphernalia already told me that.]

- At the end of your message, press 1. [Screw you.]

- Beep. Beep. Beep. etc. Beeeeeeeeeeeeeeeeeeee-eeeeeeeeeeeeeeeeeep.

- Hello, Paraphernalia. This is Jackass. Try leaving a message for yourself.

- Click. Ha!

7

"THIS IS YOUR CAPTAIN SCREAMING"

Here we have a chapter on COMMUNICATION. (Not noise, Communication. There is apparently a difference.) It is imperative these days that companies keep in constant communication with their customers, even if that means driving them crazy.

How are we to know that we are getting *Customer Service* if we are not constantly being reminded of it? So here come the announcements—a kind of looping we cannot escape in any class. That is because announcements are so cheap. Besides, what else has a Captain to do? Have a chat with the auto-pilot? Maybe it is just as well. We wouldn't want them downsizing the pilots, would we.

In trains, they simply post things. But flying is an oral culture. The airlines have to *say* everything. If these people were running the railroads, they would be giving the conductors opera lessons and having them march up and down the aisles singing refrains from Gilbert and

Sullivan: "Gentlemen will please refrain . . . from flushing toilets while the train . . . is standing in the station . . . we love you."

Or how about this one, which I quote precisely. Uncle Sam Airways was trying to leave Philadelphia for Montreal. After "some last-minute lavatory problems we are trying to resolve" (he didn't have to get *that* personal), Our Captain announced: "Another little delay. A little pin in the toe bar is broken in the tug that pushes us back. Maintenance informs me it will be about a three-minute delay. It's a shear pin. From time to time it breaks." So do my eardrums, Our Captain.

I once innocently flew Blimey Airways from Manchester to Paris, a flight that does not take quite as long as some of the immigration lineups at the John F. Kenaughty Airport. Between the announcements and the looping, I counted 25 interruptions. An average of one every three minutes! Divided Airways from San Diego to Chicago was not that bad, but for *four hours.* They used those boom LOUDspeakers, aimed directly at *my* eardrums. Time after time: "This is Your Captain screaming. . . ." When we finally got to Chicago, those things were red hot. So were my ears.

They don't talk all the time, Our Captains. There are times when they keep perfectly quiet. Like those moments before landing, when there is that terrifying roar as the plane slows down. "Don't stop here," I yell out to myself, "whatever you do, don't stop here!" Never a mummer of reply from the flight deck.

Mostly, however, the problem with announcements is getting worse, which should make solving it easier. The trick is not to reduce the number of announcements, but to increase them, slightly, to the point where they never stop. In that way, no passenger need ever be interrupted again.

All these announcements are carefully timed to catch as many of us as possible as we doze off. "This is Your Captain screaming, yet again. You will be delighted to know that we are flying over Spearfish, South Dakota. If you look out the left side of the airplane, beneath the clouds, you will see the local gymnasium."

Now think about this. In the smallest of commercial jet aircraft, only one person in four can benefit, so to speak, from such an announcement, in the largest, one in ten. Short, of course, of sending the whole can into a spin. (Do you remember that blubberhead next to me, the one with the elbows? He lifted up my armrest, bent over to have a look, and slobbered his Chateau Chirac 1943 all over me. If he hadn't been bigger, tougher, and more territorial than me, I would have hit him with my bag of dry-roasted peanuts.)

To keep everyone fully awake, entertained, and *Served,* Our Captain repeats each such announcement in seven languages. This way she/he can show off her/his linguistic ability, and find something to do while passing the time in the cockpit.

But one language is always missing: the second one of the country in question, such as Catalan in Spain, French in Canada, English in Australia. For these announcements, they use a special member of the crew—on flights to Australia, for example, someone who went to Oxford.

If this person belongs to the local independence movement, she/he will leap to the microphone and repeat the announcement as quickly and aggressively as possible, sneaking in somewhere the local battle cry. In Australia, to continue with our example, it is "Rule Britannia!" Less nationalistic ones survey the passengers very carefully. When the optimal number has dozed off again, they amble up to the microphone and go over the whole thing again, as loudly as humanly possible.

Why is it, I always ask myself at these points—probably because I am in a dazed stupor—that the second language of a country always takes so many more words than the first? Oxford English en route to Australia is the worst. "Good afternoon, ladies and gentlemen. We do hope that you are enjoying your crossing. Your Captain has taken the greatest pleasure in informing you that the continued descent of this vehicle will cause the latex to hit the macadam in barely the twinkling of an eye. Would you be so kind, therefore, as to reconnect the two sides of your safety device. (Psssst: Rule

_{Britannia!})" Funny, all I thought I heard Our Captain say was: "Hang on mates, we're headin' down."

At this point, I must make a little announcement of my own, since all of this is about *Reader Service.* If you think that we have all these tiny chapters in order to stretch out this pamphlet so that it looks like a real book, you are sadly mistaken. We have them to enable you to read each chapter between the announcements. But please, read quickly.

8
THE DANGERS OF FLYING DOWN UNDER

Every book on Management must pay homage to GLOBALIZATION—the doctrine that the world is round and that all kinds of people just like you can be found on the other side, even if they do talk funny.

"**W**elcome to New Zealand" starts a favorite line of the pilots who fly Down Under, "please set your watches back eight hours and your lives back twenty-five years." This sounded rather good to me, even in Newzinglish, so I invited daughter Lisa along.

Poor kid getting there though. Ten times going up and coming down. Up in Montreal, down in Ottawa; up in Ottawa, down in Calgary; up in Calgary, down in Los Angeles; up in Los Angeles, down in Honolulu; up in Honolulu, down in (whew!) Auckland. For the mere cost of another American college education, I could have sprung for a flight that skipped Calgary.

Ah, but the way back was so much more efficient. No matter how many ups and downs, we still arrived before we left. These are the little things I love about flying. All those hours in the airplane and no time lost at all. There we were, at John's house in Auckland, having dinner on Sunday evening. "It is hard to believe," I exclaimed, "that this very Sunday evening, at this very time, we shall be having dinner at Dick's house in Los Angeles."

But Lisa was having none of this. To this day, she cannot come to grips with the fact that she lost a day of her life on the way over—wiped out, gone forever. "But you got another one on the way back," I continue to plead, to no avail. "What if it had been my birthday?" she wails.

I need to tell you a little story about this. (You may have noticed that I need to tell you a little story about everything. Please be assured that my little stories are all true. Only the details have been embellished, to persecute the guilty.)

I was to go to Australia first. *They* were paying, namely the Aussie businesspeople who invited me to give a seminar. They got me, and I got the points: payola time! I was to join Lisa later in New Zealand, to frolic among the kiwis.

It was really quite simple. Get to San Francisco, change planes, and arrive refreshed in Sydney after another half a day, not to mention that day lost in the stratosphere. I had a few hours free between flights in San Francisco, so I arranged to meet Robert for dinner.

"Just let me check in," I say to Robert innocently.

"Can I please see your passport?" asks this Quantum Airways guy dressed up in a koala suit.

"No problem, I never forget my passport," I tell him. I eventually find it in the bottom of my bag.

"Where is the visa?" he asks.

"Visa?" I ask back.

"Visa." he answers back.

"But I'm Canadian," I answer his answer back. "The Australians are our friends. We belong to the same Commonwealth of Nations. We ask God to save our same, gracious Queen."

"Canadians need visas to go to Australia," says my compatriot.

"Bloody hell they do, mate," I reply.

"Precisely," he counters: "No problem. You can go to the Australian Consulate on Monday morning and get one."

"But this is Friday evening," I point out.

"Precisely," he recounters. "They are closed until Monday morning."

Robert and I stand there looking helpless. Robert teaches venturing at the Sitford Business School. "Do something," I plead. So Robert looks helpful.

It works. We are handed a telephone. Another Quantum person is on the line, probably also in a koala suit. "Well," he says, "you could go to New Zealand." He doesn't understand.

"Go to New Zealand!" I say. "I need to be in Australia. I know this place is full of kangaroos, but New Zealand is no mere hop away."

For some reason, he does not appreciate my hilarious sense of humor. But he does understand: "Exactly," he says. "The only way we can let you on that plane is if you are in transit to New Zealand. Otherwise, they fine us for allowing you on without a visa."

So I go back to the counter and show them my ticket to New Zealand. Ha! No good, they say, you cannot be in transit for a week. So I buy another ticket to New Zealand.

My strategy on arrival is simple. I have to miss my connecting flight. What a treat! Then, not knowing what to do with me, they may just relent, and give me a visa right there. I have to be sure, however, not to utter a word about Oxford English announcements.

In the Sydney Airport, I doodle, then amble over to Immigration. "Excuse me, sir. Will you have some time in about an hour or so? I arrived Pampered Class, which means I have all the time in the world. I would like to discuss a little problem with you. No rush. Transit lounges are such fun places to be. Besides, life is so hectic Up Over that any time we Pampered People get to relax is ever so appreciated."

Eventually, I end up in this guy's office, a Mr. Ratched. "I know your sister," I say, hoping to establish a friendly relationship. "Doesn't she work for Air Gaul?"

"Can I please see your passport?" he answers, adding much later, "It is in the bottom of your bag, muttonhead, like everyone else." Then comes the question I have been dreading: "Where is your visa?"

"Well, sir, you see, that is the little problem," I say.

"I think we shall have to send you straight away to New Zealand," he shoots back, pronouncing the last two words as if they are located beyond Hell. Drats. And I have just missed my plane. The next one is not for hours. In Auckland, I shall have to wait until Monday morning to go to the Australian Consulate. After that, I can fly back in time to wrap up my session on Monday afternoon.

Then it hits me. He said "I think." That might have meant he thought. But I entertain a more likely explanation, which is: "I have a good mind to teach you a lesson, one that you shall never forget." As if that had not already happened in San Francisco. I knew right there that the British Commonwealth of Nations was dead. "Then, when you are fully terrorized," this explanation continues, "I shall ever so gratuitously relent, so that you will *know,* not *think,* what a wonderful human being I truly am."

Do you think his "I think" meant what I thought? My suspicions are soon confirmed. He leaves the room, and another officer (no relation to the Ratcheds) sticks her head in. "Someone has been asking for you at Arrivals. I told her you won't be long." Just as I thought.

Eventually, he returns. So as not to spoil his fun, I keep perfectly calm, jumping up and down only twice. Then, on cue, he relents, grants my visa, allows me to shine his shoes in gratitude, and off I go.

Shortly after comes the realization that my bags have gone off to frolick among the kiwis of New Zealand. And so, in Sydney, Australia, do I realize my lifelong dream: I lecture to a roomful of proper executives in my dirty jeans.*

---

* Remember that slobbered Chateau Chirac, 1943?

9

IT'S TIME TO GET REALLY COMMERCIAL

Finally, we come to the chapter of all chapters: MARKETING! Marketeers (not marketers), in spite of their subtle modesty, rule the corporations, which means that they rule the world. So pay attention.

Once upon a time, in an airline's head office, a finance person bumped into a marketing person at the caviar machine. Such encounters are rare and exceedingly dangerous. In this case, nothing has been the same since. Times were tight—their proper Lamborghinis were about to be replaced by BMWs—so there was a desperate search for new revenue. After looking around carefully to make sure no one from operations was listening—people who worry about landing gear and the like—they came up with an idea. Yes, an idea!

"All those—you know, what do you call them . . . passengers—up there: they are all captive, right? All that time and money, and no way to use either. We sure can. You remember on television last night they showed these . . . what do you call them . . . advertisements. Well, we have television up there too, I seem to recall. And no mute buttons. But we do have 'Seatbelt' signs."

* * *

"Avarice Airways is delighted to inform you that the Helltown Hotel Chain and Pains Rent-a-Car are our partners in cream on the ground. We know you cannot wait to give them your money. If you do, out of the goodness of our hearts, we shall give you 'Miles!'"

Now let's put this proposition to a bit of scrutiny. Even if we accept for a moment that these airline people know something about flying, does that make them knowledgeable about sleeping and driving? True, not for a moment would I even entertain the thought that My Airline would act in any interest but My Very Own. Without doubt, they have negotiated the best possible deals for me on the ground. Why they know, just by virtue of my sitting here in Pampered Class, how terribly strapped I am for cash and how I spend every penny of other people's money with the utmost of care. Still, I do have this nagging feeling that I could get a better deal if I asked the floor sweeper.

But acquiesce, I of course do. I have been conditioned to consume, programmed to participate. Up here, in the thin air, I can't even tell the difference between the announcements and the advertisements. Imagine that. I am so stupefied by all this yakking and hawking that when a contract consecrating all my sleeping and driving to Helltown and Pains is placed before me, I sign obediently. But I must admit it was clever of them to slip it under the immigration card and say, "Sign these please, Mr. Jackass." (As usual, I put all the information in the wrong boxes. I went up instead of down—or was it down instead of up. But they got me anyway.)

Then came "Duty Fee." They call it "Duty Free." But I believe the airlines have been altogether too free with their "r's." Up here, being free of the need to charge all those government duties has enabled them to slap on all these shareholder fees. And so just as the pilots became entertainers, the flight attendants have become hucksters. And they enjoy it so!

Ah, here they come now. Reminiscent of the peddlers of old, these merchants of new push their carts down the aisles, ready to trade their booze and baseball cards for camels and goats. If you've got it, they'll take it. "For you, we have this lovely gold watch. Just the thing to double-check the lateness of the plane. A Wedgwood bowl for your cat? How about a muff for the little lady, emblazoned with a picture of our fearless leader? And mustn't forget our gold-plated gumdrops." Business has apparently become so good that some airlines are reportedly replacing Sardine Class with a full-fledged souk.

Yet, if the airlines can be faulted—something that I, personally, would be loath to do—it is not for being too commercial, but for not being commercial enough. These people are barely out of diapers compared with *real* merchandisers—the International Olympic Committee, for example, even if those guys have yet to rent out the space on their own ties. Hey, listen, if the athletes can be sponsored by sugared drinks, surely the airlines can do a deal with life insurance.

Marketeers love FMCGs. Some of them even know that it stands for Fast-Moving Consumer Goods. Well, I ask you: Fizzy drinks? Yo-yos? Throw-away pens? Come on, guys, which of these can keep up with an airplane? Get moving, marketeers.

For starters, you will have to persuade the airlines that their business is no more about moving people around than the Olympic Games are about jumping over bars. These things are about money, which means they are about sex. And that means the airlines have been missing a sure score.

Take a good look at those planes. What an image! Pregnant with potential. Except for two little problems. The wings. Those things are unbearable. The wings will have to go.

The problem is perfectly clear. The airlines have, for too long, been run by the operations crowd, who are obsessed with landing gear and the like, even with getting people from one place to another. Such a silly idea. Like believing that clothing has to do with warmth, beer with inebriation, diamonds with drilling. Treating the passengers inside these tubes as seminal is like pretending that sex has to do with procreation. That is passé! These people are markets, that's all—exploitable sources of Shareholder Value. Imagine the potency of putting these planes into the hands of the marketing people. Let them get rid of those wings, and then watch the airline image take off.

With that, the real selling can begin. Not tickets, silly; people have to buy those. Real selling. How about slot machines around the toilets, where everyone waits. Between announcements, the pilots can act as auctioneers—no further training necessary. They can auction off their insignia, autographed flight plans, full-scale models of the landing gear. How about guided tours of the wings? Squeegee kids to clean the windows? One section of the cabin might be designated "The Cabaret," where the flight attendants can get to sing and dance. CDs of the pilot's announcements could be sold. Why not vacuum-packed airline food for takeout (actually, why bother with the vacuum-packing)? Imagine pedicures in Sardine Class, to gain some space. And personalized little white bags, embossed with the crest of the Marketing Team. As we have learned from those Olympics people, the possibilities are endless—like the skies.

10

REHEATING QUANTITY

Here we have a chapter that skirts around QUALITY. The problem is that quality can't be measured—that's called quantity, although Managements often mix them up. But we know quality when we see it. Except in the rarefied atmosphere of the airplane, where we only know quantity when we see it, let alone eat it. (Notice that this is the longest chapter yet.)

So far, so good. But that is only because we have not come to the meals. Tuck in your bibs. Here they come!

We are on a plane (of course). I cannot remember where—and certainly not why. All I know is that I am sitting near the back, squashed alongside the window. They bring lunch. Cute little boxes. I get a brown one—for carnivores. The guy next to me, the one with the elbows, gets a green one—for vegetarians. (Hmmm, maybe I'll go for that armrest after all.) He finds vegetarian ham in his sandwich, but it looks curiously like my carnivorous ham. He calls over the flight attendant. "Can't be," she says. "The box is green. It must be vegetarian." He is able to make his point only because, lucky for him, the ham has not yet turned as green as the box.

Now, true, we don't always get little boxes. On flights of several days, we get little trays. People who have never flown before love those little trays. They are so adorable. The little cutlery, play knives and forks, and everything tucked into everything else, plus a spot of appetizer and a dab of dessert. Almost like real eating. And in the middle of it all, the *pièce de résistance*—the main course, all wrapped up. Can't wait to dig under that foil.

By the side is a little sealed cup of water. In this thin air, it has become a one-sided balloon. Hey, Meathead, open it carefully. Carefully! No! No! . . . All over my coloring book.

At home, I use my elbows when I eat. We're not big on strait jackets in our house. But up here, eating is ethereal. This must be how sardines eat.

I pick up the first course, a lovely little salad, two or three scraps of—yes, green—lettuce. I take off the plastic wrapping. Then I find the dressing. Now I have to put back down the salad to put on the dressing. Oh-oh. It fit there before. Can this be some kind of airline puzzle? I know, I'll put the water cup inside the coffee cup to make room for the salad. Whew! Pretty good, don't you think? Without elbows!

Reheating Quantity

I open the dressing. Whoops! "Sorry." (Serves him right for drenching my coloring book.) Now I know why they call it "dressing."

Better take out the napkin. I think I see it over there, hiding under the pepper. Whoops! Oh well, better leave it alone. I might spill something on my foot.

The fork works—sort of. Now to that *pièce de résistance*. Can't wait. I pick it up. Ouch!! What to do—quick. I'll grab Meathead's pillow; he'll never notice.

OK. Off goes that foil. Oh! Well, it isn't green.

What's he got? Sideways glance. Not to establish gender. Nothing lovely in sight. Only his fish. Hmmm. Not exactly white either. I wonder. No—better stick with what I'm stuck with. But I will keep that fish in mind next time I fly from Vienna to Istanbul.

Let's see. I just have to set it down. Oh-oh. It fit there before . . .

Anyway, you get the idea. Eating in an airplane has to be treated like playing musical chairs. Except without the music—or the chairs. Plates instead. You always have to keep one in the air. I have become a master at sleeping while holding up an empty dessert dish.

Do you think the airlines have designated jobs to make the food taste bad? (I'm told they're called "Accountants.") This has to take effort, no? Food doesn't taste this bad all by itself. I wonder if they mix up the people who buy the fish with those who age the meat. Listen, I have an idea: Make them serve airline food in the company dining rooms. A fate worse than flying.

Now that problem with the vegetarian box could never have happened in Pampered Class. If you showed them a piece of lettuce as green as the fields of Ireland and claimed it was ham, they would whisk it away in a moment, apologizing all the way from Dublin to Dubai. So if you are serious about eating, let me take you through that magic curtain into Pampered Class. Not a moment too soon, you may be thinking— foolishly.

Some years back, the airlines wrestled with a terrifying problem: How to make Pampered Class as excessive as its price. A roomful of very significant executives gathered around a table and pondered this for months. They told each other important things like: "We must distinguish our brand"; and "It is imperative that we exploit our core competence." Nobody knew what was going on.

Then, one memorable day, one of them leaped out of his chair. After returning with his cappuccino, he bellowed: "I think I've got it. Yes! Yes! We'll ply them with champagne and foie gras." His colleagues were beside themselves (where, as a matter of fact, they had been all along). After several carefully calculated moments of stunned silence, they all broke out in rapture. "Awesome!" they said, "Brilliant!" This guy is so creative, they all thought, so generous, that they could hardly believe he had gone to Be School (which should really be called Get School).

All the other airlines, in comparable fits of imagination, followed suit. And so, every goose in the Perigord and every grape in Gaul headed for cover as the race was on for fatter, bubblier, richer.

I take you now to a flight that I remember all too well, since I used to take it all too often: Air Kanuk 1867, from Montreal to Paris, Pampered Class, with the loopiest of loopers. It is getting on to 9:00 P.M., meaning 3:00 A.M. in Paris—we are almost two hours out of Montreal—and I have in front of me a starched tablecloth about a quarter of an inch thick. I am starved but must resist attacking the tablecloth because I have no cutlery. The drinks have come, I do admit. There must have been an early chief of Air Kanuk who warned in his will that if ever a morsel of food was served before the drinks, he would put a hex on all the planes. Air Kanuk could be flying Muslims to Mecca at midnight and they would still serve the drinks before the food.

Finally, it comes—the cutlery, I mean—on a trolley with specially inflated tires. Each of the six items placed before me weighs some significant fraction of a pound, designed, no doubt, as ballast for the tablecloth should a window blow out.

The food is taking so long it is as though they are out catching the fish. But I know better. So I wait patiently, much as did the member of the herd I am also about to be offered. Only four more hours to Paris. Air Kanuk's *The Ritual* is unfolding on schedule.

To tease rather than ease our hunger, they put down these little beige things before me. The French call them "mises-en-bouche," which can be roughly translated as "stick them in your mouth" or "*on* your mouth," as the case may be. I use the handy toothpicks, but no matter: they whisk away my kilos of cutlery, and replace them all, as they will do several more times before *The Ritual* ends.

(If you have come to believe at this point that I am picking on Air Kanuk, then I wish to inform you that you are perfectly correct. And I do this for a perfectly good reason. Not because Air Kanuk is a bad airline—in fact, it used to be a rather good airline, as airlines go, and its president has given me his word that, in 180 days, it will be so again—but because, from where I live, I have to fly Air Kanuk a lot. So I spend my time hating Air Kanuk. Like everyone else, because I hate flying, I hate the airline I know best.)

The glossy four-color menu was presented to me some time earlier, like a diploma at a graduation ceremony. But it offers the usual choice. Only the adjectival phrases change. But there are so many of them that nobody notices the two nouns that really matter. Tell me: Do you reheat *steak* and *fish* in your house?

Reheating Quantity

I posed this very question in a letter I wrote to the Chief of Air Kanuk. For some reason, he never replied. Maybe the answer would have embarrassed him.

Why always steak and fish (although never, absolutely never, sardines)? Why not a simple lasagna? Lasagna is so good reheated. (Curries, too. Mmmmm. I should have taken Air Hindi, even if they don't go to Paris.) Can't we once get something that tastes better than it sounds?*

Anyway, it's back to the "Grilled Fillet of Beef with Bordelaise Sauce accompanied by Green Beans rolled with Bacon, Sautéed Mushrooms and Hashed Brown Potatoes," or else the "Fillet of Salmon in a Cream Sauce with Fennel served with Braised Endive, Saffron Rice and Tomato Cup with Spinach." Like I said, steak and fish. My decision hinges on why the beef is *with* the sauce while the fish is *in* it. But they can't explain, so I flip a spoon to decide, bruising my leg in the process.

Somehow I make it through whatever it is I had— hard to tell. The cheese follows, sometime later, on its own cart. Each dainty little morsel of curdled milk is wrapped in its own little doily: Bombel from France and Velveeta from America, or at least their near equivalents, plus something blue (hopefully, intended). I am

---

* The airlines in America sometimes serve pastas, in Sardine Class at least. But that doesn't count because America is an Italian country.

supposed to make my choice like some kind of Count in a three-star Parisian restaurant. "That stuff over there," I point, with an elegant finger. I gobble it down, the cheese at least, then wait the socially correct interval for dessert. Eventually, it appears, the carts rattling down the aisle like the Grand March in *Aïda*. My choice is carefully scrutinized. "I'll take the banana," I say. No need to point. This I gobble up too. After subsequently fighting off six or eight offers of coffee, I prepare for sleep. We are still over the Atlantic. Barely.

That sleep is not long in coming. Nor in going. My Captain is soon back on the LOUDspeaker. "This is Your Captain screaming," he says, sounding like an announcer at a hockey game, although we passengers act more like mourners at a wake: "It is so exciting! We are a mere hour and a half from Paris. Wakee! Wakee!" That may be true, but we are also a mere four and a half hours from Montreal, where it is now midnight. And my stomach has not yet even come to the Velveeta.

Once upon a time, a psychologist must have worked for an airline. "You have to give them the impression that they have passed the night," he surely said, "so that they will be ready for morning on the other side."

"But that night is only two hours long, they protested." He had a ready answer: "Look what we do with rats." So the airlines have been putting us through this hoop ever since.

OK, let's be fair. We do need time to get ready. Still, at home, that takes me thirty minutes—with a shower. What can I possibly do here that would take ninety?

Then, suddenly, as I see that Grand March begin again, I remember: Breakfast! Of course; I must have breakfast, in order to wash down—really drive down—the layers upon layers of dinner. I dare not say no; I am, after all, a passenger in an airplane.

True, last night I filled out a card advising them not to disturb me in the morning. They just never bothered to collect it. Besides, there was no place to tick off:

☐ Please shut Our Captain up.

So, obedient pampered sardine that I am, I watch them begin again. Tablecloth. Kilos of cutlery. Reheated eggs, bacon, sausage, ham, mushrooms, and tomato. Something that looks like bread. I swallow it all—my way of encouraging Flight AK 1867 mercifully to end. So sad to leave. Loaded down with a trunk full of gold-plated gumdrops, not to mention breakfast over dinner, each course waiting patiently for its turn at my digestive tract, I stagger out of the can, my wallet lighter, my body heavier. Here it is that I wonder why I didn't take along that cute little white bag.

The years pass; the suspense builds. What has become of my letter to the Chief? Surely someone has read it. I will try again. And guess what? There it is, right on the menu. True, not exactly your everyday noodles: "Egg Pasta Duo filled with spinach, mushrooms, ricotta, cheddar, and parmesan cheese garnished with carrot and zucchini Bâtonnets."

Now I'll bet I know what you're thinking: He can't fool us, this Mr. Jackass. Had he left well enough alone with the Braised Endive, Tomato Cup, and Duo, we might have believed him. But sticking that circumflex over the "â" took it right over the edge.

In that case, I suggest you get hold of the Air Kanuk menu from the Fall of 1996. There you will discover the Bâtonnets duly circumflexed in both languages. (This dish was 18 words in English, 25 words in French. See what I mean?)*

Anyway, I took the noodles. How could I do otherwise? They might have reported me to the Chief, who then might have invited me to his house for a reheated dinner. "Everyone wants the pasta," our flight attendant moaned, stupefied by the fact that people on an airplane would all do the same thing. "We had to refuse three people."

Sadly, I was not one of them. For there then came the gooiest, most overcooked pasta we have ever eaten, me

---

*Actually, I lifted the descriptions of all three of these dishes from the same menu. You don't think I would keep more than one of these things, do you, let alone make any of this up? But, as I said, it doesn't make any difference because only the adjectival phrases change.

and my nice neighbor with whom I commiserated (the one with his own armrest). Why can't they just stick to the things they know how to ruin?

They don't ruin the wine on airplanes. That's for sure. No one is employed to make the wines taste bad. There are, however, all kinds of people employed to make them *sound* good. They all have advanced degrees in Creative Writing; some have even tasted the stuff.

Here, Air Kanuk was upstaged by its long arch rival, Kanukian Airlines International, the one it has since swallowed. KAI—the words were put in this order because they didn't want to be known as the KIA—was simply brilliant on the wines. The brochures, I mean; not the grapes.

The one I have before me is 17 (seventeen!) pages long and has a cover as thick as Air Kanuk's table-cloths. It is called *Cellar Secrets des Celliers* (English in one word before, French in two words after—twice as many—while in between they share the word *Secrets,* which doubtlessly raised an eyebrow or two in the Quebec separatist movement). Gracing the full-page presentation of each wine is a color picture of the vine-yard's owner. Glass in hand, he is dressed as if he spends his time stomping elegantly on the grapes.

Page 1 promises us that KAI's "wine consul-tants . . . relentlessly search for quality and grape vari-etal [I think this means variety] character . . . reflected in the innovative offerings on your flight today." Here is what the guzzlers of the booze must know about the Chablis:

> The village and vineyards of Chablis are surrounded by Kimmereidgian clay deposited there by the great flood. It is this "terroir" that gives Chablis its remarkable mineral character. The Goulley family, headed by the young energetic Philippe, has been making wine in Chablis for generations and understands clearly the risk of growing vines in Chablis. These vines are the most vulnerable in France. Philippe is a dynamic force in Chablis where he is spearheading a movement to farm organically. His Chablis is classic . . . [its] unmistakable crisp fruit aromas and mineral character abound in the aftertaste.

Philippe provides deeper insight: "My business is very traditional which means keeping still creates no progress. I strive for innovation that will work alongside tradition. We can't change the soil's nature but we can watch what we put into the soils." That's a good idea.

Two pages on, a grape guy from Australia says: "Understanding a customer's needs forms the basis of my philosophy." Smart. Why isn't this guy running an airline? His wine has "a hint of vanilla." Other wines in the brochure have "buttery flavors," "aromas of fresh plum jam," and "terrific fruit on the nose." If they could only find a wine with "the punch of garlic," they wouldn't need to serve food at all.

Still, try as they do, these Kanukians have remained in the little league. "The wine specialists who, with Air [Gaul], selected the wines we are serving you today are from Courtiers-Jurés Piquers de Vins de France. They were appointed official wine tasters to King Charles IV Le Bel of France by decree on March 12, 1322." Wow! These guys are really old! And this brochure is really suave—four pages is all they need. Not only that, but Air Gaul doesn't loop. (Mme. Ratched's idea, no doubt.) Earphones, menu, toothpaste, the works, all waiting by the seat as you arrive. A dinner tray with everything but the main course. You can start with dessert and move on to the cheese—as fast as you like. That's choice!

Still, we get the last laugh, we Kanuks. The French might get the old wines, but we get the new desserts. On one flight back home recently, Air Kanuk offered me this little package labeled "Vanilla Ice Cream Bar with Chocolate Coating." Now you're talking! Especially appreciated by those of us who suffer from a chocolate deficiency. Best of all is trying to figure out what to do with the half you don't eat. Can there be hope for flying after all?

11

> *We are into MAINTENANCE now. Remember Maintenance? It used to appear at the bottom of the chart, before all those managers pushed it off. Women may bump their heads into that glass ceiling, but try being a Maintenance man bumping your head into a concrete floor. I have been told that maintenance still exists somewhere deep inside many airlines, although, as you shall see, they do not always get it quite right.*

Once before, I must admit, I got a really good night's sleep in an airplane. Air Kanuk, no less, to London, no less, this time for all the wrong reasons.

I had to be in Quebec City one Saturday evening, followed by a full day of teaching in London on the next Monday. My only hope was to take a very early flight Sunday morning to Toronto, where I could catch a day flight to London. I take you now to the airport in Quebec City at 6:00 A.M. on a nippy day in December.

What a lineup! Both of us. Why, I wonder, do New Yorkers herd into La Gotcha Airport on a Friday evening when they could go out of Quebec City on a Sunday morning? I board—no waiting, no passports, no trunks, no armrests. The plane goes a few feet, then stops for a nice little shower. It doesn't like ice on its wings. No problem. Better it should wait than me. Then it goes a little further and comes back for another little shower. Oh-oh. Less nice. Now the plane and I are both waiting. Any thought that this may be some kind of airplane fetish is dashed by that famous click of the loudspeaker. It is Our Captain screaming. We have one of those "little problems."

Let me tell you: There is no such thing as a "little problem" in an airplane. There is a problem or there is not a problem.

* * *

Here (Your Author scribbling, yet again) I must announce a little interruption of my own. (OK, an interruption.) I must take you back to a flight to University Park, Pennsylvania, some years earlier, in a really little airplane—eight simple souls lost in the clouds.

This is going to be fun, I think to myself. For once, a real airplane. A real airline too: The pilot is a woman. [Hey! Wait a minute. Did you notice? *We interrupt this interruption to bring you a really important revelation.* I don't hate flying at all! Turns out I love flying, even when there is no one lovely in sight. It's those airlines I hate, those big bureaucracies of the sky. Is it too late to change the title of this book?]

Back in the real little airplane, we are having a nice flight so far. We sit two across, one on each side of the aisle. The other passengers must be anthropologists doing research on the distances between people in airplanes. Except for the guy next to me—a Brit on his way to visit his pen pal in Pennsylvania. No kidding. Never stepped foot in a plane before today, back in London. "You're going to love this little plane," I tell him.

OK, so I got it wrong. I hear the landing gear go down. Ever so reassuring. Then I hear the landing gear go down again. Less reassuring. Here comes that famous click. "We have a 'little problem' with the landing gear," says our pilot. Not to worry. All we have to do is fly around for an hour or so in the turbulence so that the plane can empty its fuel tanks.

In the process, most of the passengers do likewise. Finally, some justification for all those cute little white bags. A little too little for the guy diagonally opposite me, however, who seems to be on some sort of nonstop excursion. A wretched hour indeed.

The pen pal fares better. Maybe that's because he doesn't know what he's supposed to do in such circumstances.

Not to be rude, certainly not to avoid that guy diagonally across, I change seats. I head for one at the back.

It's empty there, and I once heard about planes preferring to mess up their fronts first. Besides, there's a door back there, just for me. All my life I have wanted to be the first one out of an airplane. Why not today?

There I make an important discovery, to the great chagrin of my little white bag. My seat goes all the way back, and by stretching my stomach way out, I manage to keep my fuel tanks full. But why not? Their contents don't pose a fire hazard.

Our pilot tells us that we shall be heading for Harrisburg, where there is "more equipment." Oh-oh. It's like mountain climbing, I tell myself: The worst that can happen is that I'll die.

They do a flyover so that someone on the ground can check the wheels. Apparently they look quite fine, sitting there underneath the plane, even though the control panel inside the can disagrees. So the decision is made to try to land normally.

[Did I make it? Can you stand the suspense? I'm taking bets. Even money. Write to jackass@delphi.bray.]

Here goes: Heads buried in hands—as instructed, silly—we touch down. Quite literally. It has to be one of the most delicate landings in the several hundred million years since flying began, although after that it becomes rather abrupt: we stop in eight millimeters. In the process, every bell and whistle in the plane shrieks in protest. "You should not have done that," cries one, and "Crazy bunch of cowboys in the cockpit," yells another. Why one gentle little gong would not suffice, I cannot imagine.

We disembark to discover the "equipment" in question: precisely one ambulance for each of us in the plane—an ambulance of my very own!—plus hoards of relieved firefighters. So much for that "little problem."

* * *

Our little problem in Quebec City does not get fixed. Our flight has been canceled. That is the good news. The bad news is that I can fight my way back through the storm to the hotel and finish my good night's sleep. I have been put on an afternoon flight to Montreal and then onto an overnight flight to London. The other good news is that there is no room in Pampered Class. The other bad news is that my hour of rarefied sleep is doomed, and so, therefore, is my day of teaching.

In Montreal, whine and grovel though I may, not a single pampered seat opens up. I am given a piece of paper that will reimburse me for being reduced to Full-Fleece Economy. (Weeks later, the check arrives for—I kid you not—$75. The case is about to go before the International Tribunal for Airline Atrocities in Baghdad.)

Anyway, I head for Sardine Class. And guess what? It's empty! Everyone has escaped to Pampered Class— for those Bâtonettes with their circumflexes, no doubt.

That is probably why the plane flies all the way to London with a slight downward tilt.

I walk straight to a row of three seats. I bless the fact that only two armrests need be raised. I grab a bunch of those towels they call blankets and several of those postcard pillows and down I go, arriving in the clouds before the plane.

We are blessed with a pilot who must have laryngitis. He fails to point out Iceland several thousand miles to the left, so I sleep wonderfully well, waking naturally less than an hour before landing. Still time for a shower. (What, no wake-up call?) And then, guess what? They bring me breakfast! Those kind, considerate people of Air Kanuk have thought of everything, including breakfast for those of us who may have missed dinner.

At Haltrow Airport, aware that I am on a roll, they clear away all the lines, so that for once all goes well. The only problem is the lineup to buy tickets at the Underground, which snakes back and forth like an intestine. (When you arrive at Haltrow over ground, it is best to go to London underground.*) But the gods continue to favor me, for there, right near the front of the

---

* Now they have the Haltrow Express, 15 minutes to Puddinghead Station in London every 15 minutes. Really good. Half the time it took me a few days later to get from Terminal 2 to Terminal 1 at Charlie the Gaul's Airport in Paris. Just be sure to arrange your business in the station, because sometimes you could be back at Haltrow before you can get a taxi.

line, is Reinhold. So not only do I get my ticket quickly, but I have a chance to harangue poor Reinhold all the way to London.

Reinhold works for Lifthands. I tell him about this book I am writing, on why I hate flying. Yes, I know, Reinhold tells me politely every time we meet, "You tell me about it every time we meet." And then he adds, even more politely, "I am looking forward to reading it." Ye gods! Looking forward? If Reinhold is looking forward, should I be looking backward? I mean, are they really going to let airline people read this book? You won't find me in any dim airplane for a while, I can tell you.

Anyhow, that is how I arrived at my destination, fully relaxed, only a half hour late, there to spend a wonderful day teaching. Ever since, I make sure to book Sardine Class, Seats 93X, 93Y, and 93Z.

12

Consider this to be the chapter on BENCH-
MARKING. Not marking benches, imitating.
Benchmarking means comparing your organiza-
tion to others that are better than yours so that,
at best, you can become second best—along-
side everyone else. Becoming good is another
matter. Here we ask: Can airports become, if not
good, at least almost as good as airlines?

Because the subject has already come up, let us return to airports. That is the trouble with flying: We always have to return to airports. Think of how much fun flying would be if we didn't have to return to airports.

The problem might be their individuality. Airports are so unique, so preciously different from everything around them, that you can never tell whether you are in Nagano, Napoli, or Nashville. It is as if some giant helicopter appeared one day from the Great Airport Assembly Factory in the Sky and simply dropped each given airport in its place.

It is really quite amazing that you can cross the world in a few hours and arrive in a wholly different culture without ever having to leave the comfort of Your Very Own. There may be rickshaws out there, or penguins, but don't worry: Your world is safe in here. Should you have been so foolish as to arrange a meeting outside this womb, then they leap to your rescue: A big black car—really three big black cars welded together—scoops you up and spits you straight into a hotel that looks remarkably like the one you just left on the other side of the globe. There, you hold your meeting to discuss how to adapt your chewing gum to the local culture.

Your Very Own Culture is, of course, that of the Global Manager. The Global Managers in question are, of course, those who studied economics or engineering in some country they can no longer remember and then took an MBA in America, which, unfortunately, they remember all too well. This has enabled them to fly between companies much as they fly between countries. The Global Products in question are, of course, generic: they must look the same, taste the same, and earn the same, whether in Peoria or Palermo. The Globe in question is actually a ribbon about a thousand miles wide that begins between Seattle and San Diego and runs eastward to between Buda and Pest before it picks up again in Osaka and ends in Tokyo. A long thin global village. You'd think the Global Managers could walk.

Why I Hate Airports Even More

The home of these Global Managers is, of course, the international airport. Don't get confused. Transportation is the least of it. These Global Managers meet here, they eat here, and they sleep here. You may recall that they wait here too. And above all else, they shop here. Skiphole Airport, near Amsterdam, has designated the flag as well as the motto for this club. "See. Buy. Fly." their shopping bags scream out in astounding yellow, for people who never made it past "See Jane run."

Global Managers, despite what immigration inspectors in Australia have been led to believe, are busy people. They rarely have a moment to spare, least of all to buy the products they foist on everyone else. Except in airports, where there is all this waiting to be done.

That is when fond memories arise of the family they never see—the little lady, for example, whose skin is longing for the nectars of Provence, her fingers for the minerals of Africa, her lungs for the leaves of Virginia. Lest the minds of these Global Managers wander from the wonders of such consumption, the airports are considerate enough to provide a few simple reminders—pasted on the carts, printed on the cards, penned into the carpets, plastered on the windows (in Prague, no kidding). Each and every one of these ads evokes an image of the cataclysmic coupling that will inevitably follow such offerings. Tell her you love her forever with a diamond bought as you raced from one plane to another and you may never recover from the tryst.

And what bargains! African necklaces for millions. Russian coats for thousands. French perfumes for hundreds. English cigarettes for tens. Canadian toothpicks for ones. Those of you not blessed with the Global Life may be saying at this point, "But what on earth of real use can be bought in an airport?" Staples, that's what. (No, not those things you clip papers with.) So it's off before takeoff to stock up on the essentials of life: groceries (Chernobylois Caviar, Smoked Antarctic Penguin, Beersheba Bacon); clothing (gaiters, gauntlets, galoshes); discreet personal items (rattlesnake condoms, Chateau Chirac wines, balsamic vinegar toothpaste).

The Global Manager's home away from home is, of course, The Pampered Lounge. These are such fun places to be. Just listen to the buzz: "*My* airline serves *three* different kinds of mustard with its reheated steak and yours does not." "So I booked via the Maldives— true, the long way around, but I always make a *point* of flying Air Cumulate." Lest any Global Manager miss America for a moment, the tube is glued to SeeNN—the Globe according to Georgia.

And the people in these lounges are so wonderfully friendly. Just think of all those times someone said to you: "Sure, take the seat; my coat doesn't really need it." Best of all is the décor, so novel it puts the rest of the airport to shame. Benchmarking with the hotels, no doubt about it.

Why I Hate Airports Even More

At this point, you must be wondering: If the shopping is so good, the people so friendly, the place so individualized, what exactly does this Mr. Jackass hate about airports? My answer is simple: Haltrow.

If you want to know what overgrown means, don't waste your time eating genetically modified fruits and vegetables in America. Spend a few hours at Haltrow. Taxiing to the arrival gate, for example. (You can't *fly* all the way to Haltrow.) Or transferring to Terminal 4. What these people call terminals other people call airports. I hear they are introducing scheduled flights between Terminals 3 and 4 at Haltrow.

Be careful before you take one, however. Blimey Airways' European flights go out of Terminal 1; its overseas flights leave from Terminal 4. That's easy. Now let's say you are going to Amsterdam, or Paris. I'll bet you thought these places are in Europe. Not according to Haltrow: their flights go out of Terminal 4. I know the Brits have this thing about Europe, but don't you think this is getting a bit carried away? Haltrow has since taken Moscow and Athens out of Europe. Next thing they will be claiming that Istanbul is not entirely in Europe.

In my younger, more innocent days, after having brushed up on my geography, I presented myself at Terminal 1 for a flight to Paris. Knowing Haltrow, however, I asked one of the ground persons at the door if I had it right. He looked at his buddy with a sneer and said something to the effect: "Not another featherhead look-ing for the Paris flight here at the European terminal."

If you think terminals are a problem at Haltrow, try parking. Once I got into a bus with a friend to go to her car. That bus made about fifteen stops before it finally got to the lot where her car was parked. One of those stops was for another bus—to an "overflow" parking lot. Yet we were the lucky ones: Someone told me recently he missed a flight because all those lots were full. He should have parked in Piccadilly Circus and walked.

As for the corridors, if it had been Haltrow, Theseus would still be trying to find his way out. Somewhere in this labyrinth there used to be a junction with a secu-rity machine plunked down right in the middle. Not a door in sight, no departure gate, just the intersection of two corridors. No sign was carefully placed in all four directions. So as you raced down one of those corri-dors, late for your plane, and hesitated at this junction, this guy who looked like a spider grabbed your bag and hustled you into the lineup of other victims waiting to go through the machine. Protesting that your body had barely dealt with the waves of the previous machine was of no avail.

Coming out of the machine, you still had no idea where to go. So "Excuse me," you said to another guy in uniform, standing nearby, looking bored: "The flight to Terminal 4 please . . . ?" And he answered, "Oh yes, sir, that way." The second time this happened, I screwed up my courage and popped the question: "But how was I to know? There are no signs." His answer, and I quote quite literally, was such pure Haltrow that I still kick myself for not thinking of it: "But that is why *I* am here, sir."

I figured out the system the third time I went through. As I raced to my plane, I simply chose a corridor, any corridor, without hesitation, as if I knew where I was going. They didn't get me that time, even if I did miss my plane.

I haven't seen this wonderful little junction for years. But recently, on a trip to India from Montreal, via Haltrow, I found a more than adequate replacement.

On disembarking, I receive the good news. My Air Hindi plane will be leaving from the same terminal. I only have to go to the transit area. While taking my first steps in that direction, I remember the bad news. I am at Haltrow. Hoards of people are standing before me in some sort of British queue. Hoards of anxious—in some cases, frenzied—people who have come off long overnight international flights, all apparently oozing with enthusiasm about boarding another plane just as quickly as humanly possible. Anything to escape Haltrow. But wait a minute—yet another minute: What kind of queue can this possibly be?

Some eons later, I approach the front of the line to find out. Security check. Of course. This is an airport. But wait one more minute. We all got off planes. That means we have all been checked somewhere else. The odds are quite good that none of us has hijacked our plane, let alone blown it up. True enough, but a sign explains that the British Department of Transport insists we all be checked.

Finally, I arrive face-to-face with someone official—he is wearing a uniform. He has a job to do: He must stamp my ticket. That's a good idea. "Why on earth must this security check be done?" I ask, in my stupor. "Because we have more careful checks here in Britain," he replies, adding with that certain largesse, "I know, I have traveled to some of *these* places." The Isle of Wight, no doubt.

Now, let's accept that the security checks in some of *these* places are awful. Does that mean all those people coming down with guns and bombs are waiting to use them going back up? I mean, who carries a bomb on one plane to use on another? And what about all those uncivilized airports in Europe and America that do not check their transit passengers?

OK, why blame Haltrow for its government? True. But, we haven't finished.

Beyond the stamping guy are two sets of machines to check us and our luggage. The line has now divided, half a hoard of people in each. "Why only two machines?" I call back to the stamper, who has by now faded several inches into the background. "It's only a problem in the early mornings," he shouts back in a whisper, "when there are lots of passengers—that's when the international flights come in." I understand. It's not a problem when the flights don't come in, when there are few passengers. If I flew in myself, on a carrier pigeon, I would arrive at 2:00 P.M., so that I could get through the line quickly and be sure to make my connecting flight the next morning.

I have now chosen my side. There are two people beyond the machine with wands, waiting to find our bombs. When the guy ahead of me goes through, the buzzer goes off. His pants have a zipper. One of those two people checks him very, very carefully—his glasses, his rings, everything. Half a hoard of people wait the better part of a minute. The other wand person watches all of this with equal care. No sense in bothering another passenger. Eventually, the guy does finish. But no one moves. Dazed by a night on an airplane, followed by this queue, we all wait here mesmerized, like fish before a flashlight, until we get the cue. And so, half a hoard of passengers lurch forward another few inches.

Haltrow is not all waiting. Haltrow is British. It has Class. "Dear Premium Passenger," this particularly pink envelope says. "As one of our most valued customers, we invite you to use the Immigration Fast Track Lane. . . . Simply place your completed landing card inside this special envelope and present it to our staff as you enter the Arrivals Hall. You will then be directed to the proper channel." A *proper* channel for the Pampered Class, to slip past everyone else squashed into two lines, one for ordinary Europeans, the other for ordinary foreigners.

I get it. This has to be Tony Bla's "third way" (I always wondered what that meant)—a Fast Track for the Business Class. Pay a private company more money, and the state gives you better service. What a privilege to live in such a democracy.

Haltrow is also the land of the bargain. A whole advertising campaign was mounted to tell us about it. "You don't get fleeced at Haltrow," the ads claimed. Well, not in so many words. The ads showed two pictures of some necessity of life—mink socks or whatever—one with the price at Haltrow, the other showing the same price at some place like Harolds of Serfsbridge.

Well, since Harolds of Serfsbridge is hardly my idea of a bargain basement, I checked out one of these deals—you know, did a little research. (I am not just winging this book, after all.) Instead of choosing just any old product, I selected one that is necessary for all the others. It is probably the biggest seller at Haltrow, surely the biggest money maker. I refer, of course, to money.

"Pardon me, madam," I say to this woman with "Thomas Bake" written above her head in great big letters. "If *I* give *you* a hundred American dollars, how many British pounds will *you* give *me?*" The lights flash, the computer goes round and round, the bells whistle, the gongs chime. "Fifty-four pounds and thirty pence," she says.

"Good. Now if *I* give *you* fifty-four pounds and thirty pence, how many American dollars will *you* give *me* back?"

Same routine. "Eighty-seven dollars and thirty cents," she says. Hmmmm. Why am I wasting my time writing books for millions of enthralled readers when I could be selling money at Haltrow, the bargain airport. True, Thomas has to pay for all that electricity, not to mention several seconds of this woman's time. Still. . . .

Then I notice the sign. They charge a fee. On top of the spread. Subject to the minimum (£2.50). Thomas has to eat too. Maybe $100 is not fair. I go back. I'm a high roller, after all. "Excuse me, madam, I am ever so sorry to do this again, but can we run through it once more for one thousand dollars?" She is very polite about it. "$909.39" she writes on a little slip of paper. Tom gets 45 bucks on a 1,000—each way. Why settle for 6½ percent on $100 when he can get 4½ percent on $1,000—not per year or per month, but per moment.

More recently, during another trip through Haltrow, I see an advertisement over the insignia of the British Airports Authority and Thomas Bake. "SAVE MONEY. CHANGE HERE." Finally, they have come to their senses. So I go through the routine again: $1,000, flashing lights, computer rounds, whistling bells, gonging chimes. "$885." Damn. I forgot about inflation. I forgot about home too. So I tried it in dear old Doornail Airport in Montreal. Same routine, a thousand bucks,

Canadian bucks. $813.31! Here Tom gets almost a hundred bucks each way. To be precise, 9.3345 percent, more or less. So, to change your money: FLY STRAIGHT TO HALTROW, the bargain airport.

But walk past Thomas Bake. Do not collect 126 pounds and 58 pence. Find an automatic teller machine. (Good luck. "In the terminal building, sir": a few lefts and rights, and so on.) My Canadian banking friends tell me there is usually about a $2 service charge, sometimes a bit more. The cost of the spread is 1½ percent. Add in interest at 18 percent per annum; assuming you pay your bill in a couple of weeks, that's another 0.7 percent. The total comes to 2.2 percent plus a couple of bucks. On $100 that's 4.2 percent; on $1,000, it's 2.4 percent. Better than being burned by Thomas Bake.

Maybe you think I've been a little rough on poor Haltrow, so let me take you to Vancouver Airport. At least when they take your money at Haltrow, they give you some of it back. Not in Canada, where they have learned about privatization. As a Canadian cabinet minister must have put it when this airport was privatized: "This place ain't broke, so let's fix it."

It is summertime. The lineups are horrendous. Finally, we get past check-in, only to find ourselves in a whole new line. The sign says that we have to fork over a shiny new $10 bill if we wish to fly out of the place. Money for expansion, it says. Hey, wait a minute, I think to myself, wasn't the French Revolution fought to resolve this sort of thing? I no longer have to pay those levies to transport my ideas from Fontainebleau to Paris. Why must I pay to get out of British Columbia?

The person in front of me, harboring similar thoughts, confronts the cashier. "This is outrageous. You people make me stand in line for hours to check in and then you make me stand in line again to give you money so that my descendants won't have to stand in line." On having this hypothesis confirmed by a grunt, my fellow traveler continues: "Why do I have to pay now so that you people can fix things later? This place was supposed to have been *privatized.* Don't you business types know anything about 'investment'? You want the profit, buddy, you cough up the dough." But our passenger has not realized how effectively this privatization has been done, because the cashier shoots back: "Ten bucks, granny, or your butt remains in B.C." If only there had been a Bastille nearby.

N'gara, in northwest Tanzania, is my idea of a proper airport. Even the apostrophe gives it class. The code for N'gara is '.

None of those ugly black tarmacs at N'gara. The landing strip is a beautiful rust red, a perfect match for the surrounding earth. Instead of being hidden away in some boring field, this airport is perched high up on a crest, with beautiful wide valleys all around. If, as the plane is landing, you amble up to the windshield to have a good look around, you see this wonderful view.

When I flew there, N'gara had regularly scheduled flights: the Red Cross plane went in every Monday and Thursday. You could even get one of the regular seats if they hadn't all been piled high with boxes. That way, you didn't have to sit sideways. There was no bus to the overflow parking lots at N'gara. Yet no one seemed to mind. The jeeps did have to park away from the runway, so as not to be bumped by the planes. N'gara had about as many huts as Haltrow has terminals. Each hut was high enough to stand a couple of people if it rained (in which case, the planes couldn't land anyway). But the immigration officer I saw preferred to sit, so he worked out of his car. The Tanzanian government had not yet found it necessary to have a special Track for the Pampered Class. But come to think of it, there was no Pampered Class on the Red Cross plane. N'gara does have its little advantages.

Some may think it had its little problems too. There was no airport fee, no duty fee, no Thomas Bake, no SeeNN to tell you how much money you made that day, not even any advertisements. (Hey, Global Managements, N'gara is part of the Globe too.) Worst of all, this airport was not unique. It was just like everything around it. No architectural statement at all.

It is in the hope of avoiding the mistakes of N'gara that I have included the next chapter of this book.

But first, another break

WE INTERRUPT THIS DIATRIBE AGAIN TO BRING YOU

ANNE

ANOTHER SHORT STORY, ABOUT WHY I LOVE LANDING

No shoes in sight. (Row 3 this time.) Only this beautiful head, above these elegant clothes. Same as at check-in —alone, standing well back. Well black too, from toe to head. Seemed cold then and here.

No need for sideways glances. She sits two seats over, from whence cometh the Customer Service. So he has to turneth and sayeth no every few seconds: no food, no booze, no coffee, no tea, no tea, no coffee. No interruptions? Not no nuts. Nothing to share but the discouragement. What's hers?

Water for him. The works for her, plus two bottles of champagne. One way to resist temptation.

Come to think of it, why is she flying business class from Dublin to London? On a Saturday evening? He, after all, has a (lame) excuse. The usual.

Dinner. Time for conversation. "Been cold a long time?" he could have asked. But no, he's impolite. Had enough of that routine, anyway. Besides, she's too elegant, too black. Even if he is wearing his new brown shoes.

So, while the gorgeous head gorges, beside those pillars of champagne, the bald head dozes, beneath this cloud of discouragement. Long preflight phone call. Why must it be so complicated?

He awakes. Food gone. Champagne too. Both bottles.

She reads a report. Traces forth and back across the page, a solitary finger, line by line. What in the world can possibly be so traceable? Not this. No story here.

Beneath his water sits her book. On no person's seat. Maybe she'll forget it. Then he can say, "Umm, excuse me...." And she can reply, "Why, that is ever so kind of you." Meanwhile he can't make out the title. Must be English. Can't be Gaelic, not with hair that black. She picks up the airplane magazine. Puts it right back down. Not from Hamilton apparently.

Then it happens. As his water departs, out of the black reaches an elegant hand—a hand that once seemed so cold—and gently closes their tray. Just like that.

They land. She takes the book. Can't interrupt her now. Puts a chic black coat over the elegant black clothes. Neatly hands him the bundle of coat he had dumped above.

They wait. Can interrupt her now. "Funny how people are so anxious to get out of airplanes, yet they are in no rush to leave trains." Not funny at all, let alone clever. She smiles nonetheless, a warm white smile.

Out they go, she first. He grabs a spare cart, dumps in his heavy briefcase. Down they go, along the corridors of Haltrow. A moving sidewalk appears on the left. She goes right. Walks fast, smart. Smart enough, but not fast enough. He comes out ahead. She walks faster, smarter. Passes him. Another moving sidewalk. She goes right again. (Will she never learn?) He slips out ahead, into a long narrow corridor. No chance to pass now. Ha!

Click, click, click, go those smart black shoes, not so well back. Haunting sound. Click, click, click. No one else within miles. Just that memorable click, click, click.

A carousel appears. They wait respectively. "Is this where the baggage comes from Dublin?" he asks. "Dublin? How should I know? I've just come from Rio," she could have answered, freeing herself from all this. But no. "Yes," she says. "It usually comes in on this one." She moves closer to talk. Now they're flying, these two, all alone, still out of sight.

His bag comes out. He puts it on the cart and waits. Her bag comes out. She puts it by her feet and waits. They wait respectively, talking respectfully. "Is that your only bag?" she asks eventually. "Yes," he answers. "Me too," she says. He offers her bag a place on his cart. Thus they depart arrivals.

In the main hall, he asks where she is going. "West London," she answers. He tells her where he is going: "Is that West London?" She thinks so. A taxi will be shared by all.

But first she must make a call. A cellular phone appears, black, unlike her disposition. No one home. "I'm sorry to have kept you waiting," she says.

Anne

"Do the Irish always apologize for everything, like the English?" he asks.

"Yes," she answers, with a hint of brogue, "except that we mean it!" He does love the Irish. He means it!

Into the taxi they go, lady in black in the black cab, followed by man in brown. New shoes. Lots to share (without the discouragement). She loves Dublin. Has spent her life there. Does seem to escape to London for what's left of the odd weekend, however. He just spent two days in Dublin and loved it too. Fate? No. Never strikes twice in the same book.

And that damnable question; must ask that damnable question. She runs a facial salon in Dublin Fair City, to make the girls there that much more pretty. Other girls, even if she was out of diapers back then. Has six employees, plus five part-timers. Works long hours. He writes, he tells her, including a book called **Why I Hate Flying**. (He tells everyone he is writing a book called **Why I Hate Flying**.) He illustrates. She laughs. "So that's why you didn't take the food. You only drink water in airplanes." Ah so, more than gender has apparently been established by all concerned. Must be the new shoes. Out of sight.

She tries the phone again. Still no answer. Serious happenings now. Supposed to visit friends. Left the address behind, at the shop. A new address, off Oxford Street. Can't be many of those.

Later, friends become "Peter." "I know Peter," she says, "he's sleeping it off."

As the miles tick, the situation worsens. Well, actually it improves—the journey if not the destination. More calls. Still no Peter. Leaves a message. What to do?

He gets an idea. (!!) "Maybe we can find his address in the phone book." Perhaps cabby can call: "Excuse me, cabby...."

"What's his name?" cabby asks.

"Peter!" he announces proudly.

"Ah, one of the apostles then," shoots back this man who has been selected for the journey (not the destination).

Now what? All good things must come to an end, that's what, though no one is rushing. She's in great glee, he's freshly invigorated (What, him discouraged?).

Cabby is enjoying it all too (while the meter runs). What a team!

"Where off Oxford Street?" asks cabby. Not sure: "I think it starts with a B," says the lady in black, who must have a name. The street has a name. "Berners," the cabby flings back. "I think that's it!" she replies with equal discrimination. Can't be more than several hundred flats there. "It's near the corner," she had said.

It must have been at this point that he asks if she drank both bottles of champagne. "No, I put one away," she replies.

"OK, then you're forgiven," he says. But not for being delightful.

Come to think of it, why must all good things come to an end?

Cabby suggests Peter might be waiting at Terminal 2. "You came in at Terminal 1. This flight usually comes in at Terminal 2."

Which flight, cabby?

"Not Peter," says the lady without a name: "I know Peter. He's at home, sleeping it off."

Ever to the rescue, cabby suggests a sleeping bag, laid down off Oxford Street. Until Peter sleeps it off. But where to find a black one elegant enough to grace a body such as this?

They get to his hotel. Good thing must now end. Blacker hair waiting upstairs. Can the concierge help? In they go. Concierge tries the phone book. No luck. No Peter listed off Oxford Street.

He must go. How will the good thing end? Suddenly a shout: "Peter!" The hungover apostle has answered the phone. She does know Peter!

She shakes his hand vigorously, thanking him profusely. Then she shakes his hand vigorously again, thanking him more profusely. She means it! She's Irish. They share cards—his numbers on his, her numbers on his. (She can't find her cards either.) Then she shakes his hand more vigorously still, and off she goes. Just like that.

Oh yes, her name. She does have a name. Anne. No kidding. She said Anne. So later he traces the story after all, An N, on the back of An A. Mad scribbling— well remembered.

13

RULES FOR DESIGNING THE PERFECT AIRPORT

Believe it or not, this chapter presents a MISSION STATEMENT. It just looks like a Policy Manual. Most Mission Statements are short, pithy, and meaningless. This one is long, pedantic, and meaningless. Most Mission Statements are created from a vocabulary of 29 words, including "inspire," "dynamic," "truly," and "peopleareourgreatestasset." This one is created from 29 truly dynamic inspirational ideas. Humilityisnotitsauthor'sgreatestasset.

[This is Your Author writing. This chapter is based on a document smuggled to me by a disgruntled airport employee, admonished for having made a passenger's life easier. I could get into trouble for publishing this document—the airlines have ways of losing luggage, you know. So please promise not to show it to any airport person. Should you refuse to promise, please read it anyway, because once finished, you will be in no danger of showing it to any such person. Should you be such a person, too bad for you. Please note further that this chapter should not be read in an airplane. It is much too long. You would be interrupted constantly. It has been designed to be read in an airport. I am sorry that it is so short.]

Let us be perfectly clear at the outset: Airports do not exist to get passengers to airplanes. That is a myth perpetuated by generations of advertising campaigns. If you believe this myth, you will understand nothing that follows.

Airports exist for two reasons: (1) to maximize Shareholder Value along the path to the gate, which, alas, must eventually be reached by most passengers; and (2) to gratify the glee of the groundies. [A groundie is a groupie who works for an airport.]

For some reason, people about to be hurtled into space arrive at airports under conditions of great anxiety. They are worried about missing their planes and even more worried about not missing their planes. The purpose of an airport is to convert these conditions of great anxiety into states of sheer terror, from which the owners can profit while the groundies get entertained. Most airports have made a heroic start in this direction. But a great deal remains to be done. Hence this document.

Rules for Not Getting Near the Place

1. It goes without saying—hence, we say—that the more terminals the better, and the greater the distance between terminals the better. Where distances are short, we recommend engaging an intestinal surgeon to lay out the roads between terminals.

2. Never reveal what goes on in the different terminals. It is nobody's business but your own. This is especially important if you have succeeded in randomizing the flights out of the different terminals so that no one can figure out what is going on. If forced to post explanatory signs on the incoming highways, be sure that they can be read by the arriving passengers, so long as they walk slowly.

3. To maintain the confusion, it is mandatory that travel agents be trained never to print the number of the terminal on the ticket. Fortunately, this has not been a problem, except among local agents, who do not seem to get the idea. But this is acceptable because the local passengers usually know what is going on. Should any other passenger be foolish enough to call the airport for such information, especially at long-distance telephone rates, follow the "best practice" of the airlines and answer the telephone immediately, with a message, repeated every seven minutes: "We appreciate your business."

4. Run transfer buses between the terminals on a regular schedule—for example, on the odd-numbered hours. Post the routing in tiny little

letters above the windshield, perpendicular to the boarding passengers. Ensure that the buses make regular stops wherever a passenger has been spotted at least once during the past decade. However, forbid the buses to stop where numerous passengers normally wait, because that will only increase the amount of pushing and shoving. It is a good idea, as at Terminal 1 of Charlie the Gaul's Airport in Paris, to have the bus doors open against a concrete wall, opposite the terminal door.

5. Make terminal parking as convenient as possible. Charge it at $20 per minute. "Long-term parking," so named for the time it takes to get to the terminal building, should be provided at a fraction of this rate ($\frac{3}{4}$).

Rules for Not Rolling into the Place

1. Luggage carts are particularly problematic, so a number of rules must be strictly adhered to. The most important rule is that every cart must have one wheel perpendicular to the other three. Any passenger who complains can be told about the difference between a luggage cart and an economist: only one has a mind of its own. Such jokes are to be encouraged from time to time in this otherwise proper atmosphere.

2. Carts may be provided in two ways: (a) *free-of-charge,* still favored in much of Western Europe

and most of Canada (socialists, all); and (b) *full-of-charge*, which is popular in more enterprising America. Only (b) carts should be placed in convenient locations—for example, where passengers arrive at the airport. Putting the free-of-charge carts inside the terminal building, at the far end, enhances the impact of the cart jockeys. Never underestimate the terrorizing effect on passengers of having someone who cannot see ahead pushing a half-kilometer snake of carts through a crowded airport.

3. Under no circumstances must these carts be designed to hold anything but small, rectangular suitcases. People who travel with large soft packs, skis, bicycles, and other awkward luggage must be punished by sarcastic looks from their fellow passengers as their prized possessions crash onto the floor. We understand that there have been demands by some passengers to install rubber tubes all around these carts, as on bumper cars at amusement parks. *We, the people of airports, are not amused.* This is a serious business. We recommend barbed wire.

4. Finding the carts is one thing; actually using them is quite another. Security Control plays an important role by forcing passengers to vacate their carts before they have barely begun their roll to the gate. The following we especially appreciate: The fact that people find these carts

useful for their one-minute walk to Security Control is no indication that they will find them useful for the many-minute walk to the gate. Let the passengers check everything, or else travel light—they can always eat cake at duty-fee.

5. Escalators are to be favored over elevators; they also interrupt the trip to the gate. But elevators can actually play the same role. The idea is to locate them in obscure spots, around corners, carefully placing them to allow the ingoing carts to block those coming out. Each elevator should hold precisely 1.8 carts. The elevator doors used to be wired with a special device that closed them just as soon as the outgoing carts departed. The new, improved "Bulldog" design keeps them open just a bit longer, so that they can seize the arms of the entering passengers and hold them for agonizingly long periods of time before closing with gradual determination.

Rules for Not Checking into the Place

1. Numerous opportunities exist to aggravate those passengers who persist in getting to check-in. Best is to have one single line, at least for Economy Class, surrounded by empty lines for the Business Class, the First Class, and the Upper Class, each with several agents filing their fingernails. To design this line, bring back the aforementioned intestinal surgeon. The trick here is to have numerous turns so tight that every cart that goes around the bend has to be discarded.

2. Contrary to what you might expect, we do not favor long waiting periods in the check-in lines. The trick is to keep those lines moving as steadily and as imperceptibly as possible, so that the passengers never get to put down their bags and rest, or, better still, must immediately pick them up again. This "Check-in Shuffle" also looks a lot better than the "Baggage Jerky." For those smart alecks who leave their bags at one bend in the snake line to pick them up on their way back, two solutions present themselves. The British blow up the bags on the spot. But this, frankly, is messy. We favor the American solution, which simply leaves the problem to all those (Robin) hoods who roam their airports.

3. When—and if—the passengers reach check-in, offer them a large number of luggage tags in two styles: glossy and waxed paper. Provide felt-tip pens by which to smudge the fingers and render the writing illegible. The tips of these pens should be fat, to ensure that the tiny little boxes on the cards are fully filled in.

4. With regard to announcements, do not follow the airlines' lead. Airline people talk too much, too loudly, and, especially, too clearly. One option is to forbid announcements altogether, especially in shops and restaurants. Research has shown that people who miss their planes buy more airport merchandise than people who do not. Another option is to allow announcements wherever the acoustics are especially bad. (This leaves considerable room for maneuver in airports.) A third option is to encourage announcements so numerous that they all blend into one continuous blast. Chicago's O'Roar Airport, whose announcements are thunderous, jarring, and unrelenting, is to be especially commended in this regard. Thought should also be given to the installation of tiny television sets with massive speakers, locked onto perfectly banal stations. (Here the choice is vast.) People should not be allowed to think in airports, let alone relax.

Rules for Not Getting to the Gate

1. Design the course to the gate much like the North American aboriginals welcomed their prisoners; simply replace the tomahawks with stores. Where the space for stores is limited, consideration should be given to the elimination of one or more of the runways.

2. Do **not** tamper with Security Control; its present status is about as perfect as it is ever going to get. Most airports have by now installed the new "Either/Or" equipment. On the "hair-trigger" setting, these machines can pick up a penny; on the "Pb" setting, an empty foot-long artillery shell smelling of gunpowder gets through.* The former setting is to be preferred, not for safety reasons—that is the airlines' problem, not ours—but because it provides unlimited opportunities to humiliate the passengers. After they have emptied their pockets and removed their coats, watches, glasses, and pistols, not to mention the rings from their ears, noses, and throats, and have still failed the test, send them through once more—without their belts. When the buzzer goes off again, announce that the zipper in their pants is causing the problem.

3. Where the distances to the gates are short, consideration can be given to the installation of moving sidewalks, but only after all of the possibilities for shopping have been thoroughly exhausted (not to mention all of the passengers). Make sure that these sidewalks run occasionally. In England, where people are trained to stand well over to the right, design the belts to be one

---

*It's me, Your Author. Sorry to interrupt. You may think they have actually gone over the edge here, and I cannot imagine how they found out. But I participated in a ceremony in Sweden once, in which they shot off such a shell, which they then gave to me as a memento. A few days later, for reasons I cannot remember (maybe I was doing a security check of security checks), it was in my hand luggage as I left an unnamed Channel Island that sounds like a cow. Those several pounds of metal passed the search undetected. Most reassuring. (True, it was only a hand search. Maybe they thought it was a milk container.)

centimeter wider than two carts. Elsewhere, wider sidewalks are acceptable, since they give everyone a chance to spread out. Japan offers particular opportunities in this regard. In Tokyo, people stand to the left; in Osaka, to the right. Happily they travel to each other's cities. Prizes can be offered—reheated Kobe beef, for example—to those who confuse their fellow passengers the most.

4. Gate area design has always been an awful problem. But we believe it has now been solved. Carefully calculate the most probable number of passengers for the flights out of each gate, and then provide exactly one seat less. When fewer passengers appear, appropriate signs can be posted: "Seating for passengers and their hand luggage." Apparently, problems have been reported in these places during the long delays caused by weather disturbances. How low can these passengers get? Immediate steps must be taken to replace all carpeting with volcanic pumice.

5. The skyways that lead passengers from these gate areas straight on to the airplanes provide one last shot at the passengers, so please use them carefully. These have been installed against our better judgment; we never understood what was wrong with having to fight gale-force winds and driving snowstorms to get to the airplane.

Too late now. Still, these skyways have too much character. They should be toned down, to be consistent with the lovely decor of the rest of the airport. In actual fact, we favor shuttle vehicles over skyways and walking. The passengers apparently adore them—one need only observe how anxiously they wait to get inside—and so do we: they provide two additional periods of waiting. Shape these vehicles like a pear, so that most of the space is at the back. Maybe that will move the passengers along. To those who fail to see the logic of standing well back, so as to allow everyone else to board the plane first, rent boxing gloves.

6. We recommend one last desperate effort to garner a little more Shareholder Value from your cherished Customers. Just as they are about to board the airplane, offer them a copy of that wonderful book *Why I Hate Flying,* duly discounted because you have torn out Chapters 12 and 13.

Rules for Not Getting Them Back

1. They all come back, you know. Just as things that go up must come down, people who go out must come back in. The rules here, about skyways, transfer vehicles, carts, and the like, are much the same as those for people going the other way. But special opportunities abound here as well. For example, the full-of-charge carts placed at the points of international arrival can take absolutely any form of local currency. This ensures that the local citizens—the ones who vote—are well looked after. Of course, some, having been abroad for more than a couple of days, may not have precisely the right coinage in their pocket. But, frankly, airports have no responsibility for such people. If money for these carts was not the first thing on their minds when they left, the hell with them.

2. At Arrivals, toilets are to be avoided wherever necessary. Plumbing, too, is a messy business. Where these must be supplied, hide them in obscure corners. For every male urinal, supply exactly one female stall. The women can thus learn to hurry up and not keep their male companions waiting.

3. The first currency exchange must appear after the full-of-charge carts. We suggest that the little cubicles now used be replaced by camel-skin tents, within which specially trained people can say things like: "For you, for that lovely little pound, I propose $1.25—Canadian. That is my next-to-final offer." Automatic teller machines can be installed in the villages near the airport.

4. Bear in mind that visitors' first impression of your country will be formed at Immigration Control, so great care must be taken in designing this area.

Rules for Designing the Perfect Airport

Fortunately, three models have already been well established, each with its own endearing features, wonderfully representative of the culture from whence it has come. (There is a fourth model that we reject unequivocally.)

- *B: The British Cue Model.* Britain is, of course, the land of the queue. These people love to line up, even when they have nowhere to go. British airport queues are carefully designed to snake back and forth, until they are ready to dispense their passengers to the immigration officers one by one. Over to one side is a battery of these officers, all lined up eagerly awaiting their next victim. A passenger may notice one official coming free and make a move. At this point, The Hand appears, and clamps the shoulder. The Hand belongs to the Guardian of the Immigration Gate, installed to make sure that no passenger begins the trek to an immigration officer until the passenger leaving has hit full stride. These Guardians live for the moment when they can say, "Number 141, please." Should a passenger dare to say, "But number 14 is coming up and it's only a three-minute walk away," she/he is punished by having to wait for number 144, where the officer is processing a family of fourteen from Afghanistan. This, you see, is one queue that can only be left on cue.

- *F: The French Bypass Model.* In a certain manner of speaking, the model favored in France is more efficient. The line has been developed—well, evolved really—much like a funnel. The French do not appreciate long lines. This one has thus been whittled down to three meters in length. It has, however, spread to 312 meters in width (the hall being 300 meters wide, its walls at each end 6 meters high). The thousands of people waiting to wave their passports at the disinterested immigration official simply engage in that famous French sport known as *The Bypass.* They keep moving over to gain advantage over their compatriots. (In the French language, "crowd control" is an oxymoron.) This, of course, poses a problem for those people in the middle. But that hardly matters, since none of them is French. Indeed, rumor has it that a couple has been trying to get to the front of the line at Disorly Airport for three years now. Brits, apparently. (We must point out here that the Fast Track for the Business Class at Haltrow Airport is the polite British version of the French Bypass Model.)

- *A: The American Challenge Model.* The United States has faced a wholly different problem. Ever since the closing of Ellis Island, a search had been under way for another method to process immigrants. The solution worked out

Rules for Designing the Perfect Airport

at New York's John F. Kenaughty Airport is nothing short of brilliant. It has virtually privatized this most public of services. America is, of course, the land of survival of the fittest. So this very concept has been designed right into the arrival lines at Kenaughty. Government officials need no longer even screen the incoming passengers. Anyone who actually makes it to the front of an immigration line at Kenaughty Airport is automatically granted citizenship on the spot.*

- *c:* We stand unalterably opposed to a fourth model—so much so, we refuse to italicize it, let alone give it capital letters: the canadian separatist model. Like so much else in that unfortunate country, this form of crowd control may work perfectly well in practice, but it simply does not work in theory. As people arrive—for example, at the Montreal Doornail Airport—in

---

* It's me again, with another little story. A couple I know were waiting for the wife's grandmother at this airport. The elderly lady was coming to America for the first time, from Belgium. When she finally came out, it was clear to them that she had been crying. Her granddaughter had asked her to bring some special Belgian baby powder, which she had repacked into some nice little plastic bags. She was stopped at customs—Belgian great grandmothers are particularly dangerous people—and a search produced these bags. The guy then put her through a third degree. When she could not name her Grade 3 gymnasium teacher, things got worse. Why the guy did not just try the stuff—you know where—we can only guess. Finally, he let her go. Now I ask you: Which one was the dope?

typical canadian fashion they are allowed to separate into various lines. English and French-speaking canadians can even end up in the same line. This means that when they talk about pain and pois(s)on, nobody can tell whether they ate well or had a terrible time. Moreover, people are continuously separating from one line and joining another. (These canadians can never make up their minds.) No clamping, no bypassing, no challenge. Why can't canada just behave itself and copy Britain, France, or America, as it always has? (At Farita Airport, less than a one-day trip from Tokyo, they have installed the canadian separatist model for the locals and the British Cue Model for the foreigners—an interesting twist.)

5. Passengers lucky enough to get past immigration control face the incomparable joy of baggage arrival. Just picture them all anxiously awaiting the return of their prized possessions, ready to spring to life with the first movement of the belt. That is why the belt should be started as early as possible. Send nothing for as long as you can, and then offer the occasional suitcase left over from an earlier flight. And do not forget to install several of those luggage staining machines along the inside transit belt.

6. One thing we find wholly unacceptable is the point of baggage arrival. This is absolute chaos,

with passengers lined up every which way, falling all over each other and breaking toes and ankles to save their luggage as it comes crashing down. What a disgraceful waste. We urge every airport to set up coliseum seating in this area and sell tickets as well as popcorn and raw meat. Imagine the roar of the crowd as one of those traviators grabs a bag and engages in that famous "Samson swing."

7. Never keep anyone waiting for luggage who has nothing else to do. Always keep everyone waiting for luggage who is in a desperate hurry. The latter can be identified by their incessant use of mobile telephones, the former by their habit of waving, throwing kisses, and acting out the events of their entire vacation to the admiring crowd behind the fogged-up window.

8. Make sure that the Customs Office trains its inspectors never to stop anyone wearing a shirt and tie. Such people would never dream of doing anything dishonest. They can also be dangerous—many know politicians. In the presence of a label that reads "Diplomatic Corps," Customs officers must be instructed to turn around and cover their eyes with both hands.*

---

* Me, one last time. This one is too good to miss. I rarely get stopped at customs; I must look dangerous, even without a tie. But once I did, and it can teach us all an instructive lesson. Remember that shell in a

9. Priorities must be established among the various available forms of ground transportation. Car rental companies come first. They pay good rent. Buses come last: they must stop—well, slow down really—at the extreme end of the terminal building. Train the bus drivers, when asked if their bus goes to this or that place, to mumble "Maybe." (They learn this very quickly.) In between come the taxis. These offer a golden opportunity for that famous double whammy, a marvelous trick perfected by many airports around the world: passengers can be made to wait significant fractions of hours for taxis that themselves have been waiting significant numbers of hours. It is quite simple. The cabs must pull up in a single line and load one at a time. Passengers who try to sneak down to the next taxi can be sent back to Immigration. After each

---

previous footnote, the one that smelled of gunpowder? Well, I was in that Channel Island that sounds like a cow, not to wash my money, but to go sailing. We ran into a slight breeze of several hundred kilometers an hour and nobody warned me about the dangers of going below deck. So there I spray painted the cabin, but not in a color anyone appreciated, as well as some of my clothing. I had to leave for Canada right after—no time to wash what did need laundering. Asked by the Canadian Customs inspector what I had in the bag that he was in the process of opening, I told him. He thanked me profusely, sealed it tight, and sent me on my way immediately. "Hey, I want to tell you about this Swedish artillery shell too," I called out, "not to mention all my boxes of gold-plated gumdrops?" He just would not listen. You might consider this the next time you find yourself stopped at customs.

car has been seen off with a wave, the next one is allowed to pull up. In this way, the whole line moves forward in what airport people call "The Dance of the Lurching Cabs." In a nice twist, one airport in London that will remain unnamed holds its taxis in a parking lot four miles away from one of its many terminals. No sooner is the current stock of cars depleted than the dispatcher heads straight for the telephone to call up a fresh supply.

On this happy note, we complete our Rules for Designing the Perfect Airport. We apologize for having gone to such lengths, but airports, you no doubt appreciate, require a great deal of Management—as does everything else on the face of this earth—and off it, for that matter.

14

GENUINELY SCRAMBLED MANAGEMENT

Every book on Management must have at least one chapter on MANAGEMENT. Even management schools sometimes have a course on Management. Otherwise, how could their graduates expect to manage everything? Management must be in touch, so to speak; it must hear from its Customers. That is why it has MARKETING RESEARCH, which enables them to hear from their customers without ever going near one. After all, customers can ask nasty questions; some even write nasty books. In this nasty chapter, a customer who has tried to tell Marketing Research what he thinks of Management tells Management what he thinks of Marketing Research.

What exactly is the problem here? I mean, how does all this happen? Airline managers fly, don't they? Airport managers use airports too, even if only to get to their offices.

Does anyone here remember E-stern Airlines? Please raise your hand, if your arthritis is not too bad. It used to be the biggest airline in the world. Stock market analysts will pull out all kinds of fancy graphs to tell you what went wrong. Don't believe a number of it. E-stern went belly up because of the scrambled eggs.

"You've got to be kidding," I tell the flight attendant who has just served me these things they call scrambled eggs on a morning flight from Montreal to New York. "I've never eaten anything this bad, even on an airplane."

"I know, we keep telling them, they won't listen," she says.

How can this be? Had these bosses been running a funeral home, I might understand. But flying is one business in which you can share your customers' experiences. If those bosses had bitten into those eggs just once, they would have been off the plane the next morning. So where was the big brass?

Did you guess? No, not off in space somewhere. While I was back here choking on those ostensible eggs, they were right up there in First Class, feasting away. "The biggest executive dining room in the world" is how the big boss of SASsy Airlines, in a moment of truth, once described First Class to me. He claimed that most of the occupants were there on airline business. What a good idea! Why go even Pampered Class when you can have a place in the plane all to yourself? With properly scrambled proper eggs.

Blimey Airways is very careful about its scrambled eggs—and about reminding us that it is "The World's Favourite Airline": among the stock analysts, at least, in the good old days, at least.

Once I was waiting at Haltrow Airport for my luggage. A Blimey Airways *Marketing Research Person* appeared, with a clipboard. Oh-oh. I looked around for somewhere to hide, but all I could find was my cart. No bathroom in sight. She descended upon the passenger next to me. After a battery of banal questions came this little gem (I quote precisely): "Was the pilot genuinely interested in the passengers?"

Why had I hidden? Why, for once, could it not have been me? "Marketing Research Person," I was dying to say, "was the Blimey pilot genuinely interested in flying the blimey plane?" The guy who flew that Red Cross flight to N'agara was genuinely interested in flying the plane. He owned it. He was genuinely interested in the passengers too: he shared his bottled water with us. No Blimey pilot ever did that with me.

Another time, the Marketing Research Person descended on me. Haltrow was quiet—it must have been 4:00 A.M. on a Friday the 13th. I had checked in quickly and was sitting all alone at the departure gate with too much time on my hands. I didn't see her coming until it was too late to hide under my cart.

Her questions were numerous, but every single one of them concerned the check-in. You might have thought she was interested in my reaction to it. Not at all. She was interested in circling numbers on her sheet of paper. Well into this ordeal, I blurted out in frustration: "Listen, the whole thing took maybe two minutes; we've already been here discussing it for more than ten." She would have none of this; she knew I had nowhere to go. So she continued, like one of those elevator doors in airports. After several more questions, I pleaded: "It wasn't awesome or awful; she took my ticket and gave me a boarding pass." Did the woman smile, she wanted to know. Actually, her query was: "Did she smile naturally or was it a forced smile?" (If you think I am making any of this up, then you have never been Marketing Researched.)

So I tried another tack. "Well, you decide. Her cheeks were slightly rounded, her mouth was open a millimeter or two, and she did make eye contact for that mandatory millisecond." She glared at me and circled #3 on her sheet. "But her eyes did not sparkle," I continued. "You must do something about this. Perhaps a special Eye Sparkling School next door to the Elocution School for pilots." She did not compensate with her own eyes. Thankfully, my flight was called and I dashed away to give back that boarding pass.

I long for the day when I shall be descended upon by a Marketing Research Person who wants to talk about Marketing Research Persons.

Genuinely Scrambled Management

Actually, I am genuinely interested in finding an airline that is *genuinely* interested in *us*—the people they call *Customers*. One that smiles naturally upon us with sparkling corporate eyes.

To all the rest, I wish to say: Who do you think you are, calling me a *Customer?* The nerve of you. I am a *person,* with endearing qualities and obnoxious ones. I love and hate, or, more to the point, I can be loveable and hateable. You look at me—brown eyes, potentially shining that can get glazed over, full of excitement or boredom—and all you see is *Customer,* or "Mr. Jackass," some means to maximize your Shareholders' Value—at the expense of all other human values. You seem to think that you need to call me *Customer* to treat me decently. I think it demeans me.

Please treat me as I deserve to be treated. Insult me if I insult you. (Boy, would that make flying interesting now that the book is out!) At least that would show respect for me. Then I can respect you too. If you can see beyond *Customer,* maybe I'll even be able to see beyond *Airline.*

15

WHY I REALLY HATE FLYING

This chapter concerns STRUCTURE. Structure means replacing human beings with Human Resources. Treating these Human Resources as categories ensures that they do likewise to those categories who sit in the seats. Now structure must be changed every few weeks: what is the point of being a manager if you cannot constantly be Reorganizing something. (Recall that we live in times of great change, even if managerial ties do remain knotted.)

So, would you really like to know why I hate flying? You seem to have been patient (apparently—or else long gone).

It all came out recently. Over Africa. Air Gaul, without a Ratched in sight. Such an innocent question, really. During breakfast. On top of dinner.

"Would you like the omelet or the poached eggs?" she asks pleasantly, with just a hint of sparkle in her eyes. She pronounces it clearly, even with all those extra words in French. Not theomeletorthepoachedeggs. Still, it hits me, right then and there. It's those categories. Everything is so categorical up here in the sky. Even me. Especially me, like everyone else. Up here, I'm not a person. I'm a category.

Don't get me wrong. I am not complaining that the airlines treat me like a number. I wish they would attain that level of individuality. I am a category, called *Passenger,* worse still, *Customer.* Even if they do sometimes call me "Mr. Jackass."

Airlines are obsessed with categories. "Jamormarmalade," "jamormarmalade," "jamormarmalade" recited an attendant to everyone as she went down the aisle like some sort of dispensing machine. And then there are those categories for the miles—Diamond, Prestige, Maharajah, and so on. And those categorical questions at check-in. "Have you left this bag unattended at any time since packing it?" (Yeah—it was in the back of the car on the way to the airport.)

There is a special word for organizations obsessed with categories: Bureaucracy. Bureaucracy is not about tape that is red or people that sit on their butt. Bureaucracy is about categories. Airlines are the most categorizing organizations off the face of the earth.

Why I Really Hate Flying

Bureaucracies are also about controls. And boy, are airlines and airports about controls—from the highways in to the flying out, the herding, the squeezing, the checking, the selling. Imagine a ticket agent who smiles voluntarily, a pilot who is genuinely interested in keeping quiet, a skyway with paintings of the children of the ground staff.

If you read the airline magazines, you know that those great gurus of Management have declared bureaucracy dead. We live in an age of turbulence, they keep telling us. Actually, I haven't noticed. Things seem pretty calm up here in the sky, pretty calmly categorical, in fact. Maybe those gurus never travel in airplanes. Or else, as usual, they fly several miles higher than anyone else's experience. Down here, if nothing else, bureaucracy is alive and flying high.

In my day job, when not flying, I study bureaucracy. There I am supposed to understand—be sympathetic, apologize for them. I used to write things like "The larger the system, the more formalized its behavior" and "The more regulating the technical system, the more formalized the operating work, and the more bureaucratic the structure of the operating core." Got it? (I can supply page references upon request.)

That means if we want it big, and we want it calm, we had better take it bureaucratic. And if we don't like Sardine Class, if we want to go like a dolphin, then maybe we should buy a wet suit.

So perhaps we shouldn't blame them, those flying people of the skies. They have to do it all, these Human Resources, flight after flight, day after day, "Passenger" after "Passenger." It can numb the senses. Maybe we should instead celebrate those human beings of the airplanes and airports who can get beyond the categories. And beyond the pretentiousness. Like that Blimey flight attendant who turned up on my flight out of London the day after he was on my flight into London. He was genuinely interested in seeing "Mr. Mintzberg!"—a name he genuinely remembered. (Good thing I didn't register as Mr. Jackass.) He was even genuinely sorry that they were out of the newspaper that they were out of the day before. So here's to you, the human beings of flying who manage to remain human.

And this brings us back to that nice flight attendant on Air Gaul, the one with the omelet/or/poached/eggs over Africa. Still not a Ratched in sight.

I take the omelet. She smiles: I think she is genuinely interested in my choice. If so, she is a better person than I shall ever be. Then she asks if I want coffee or tea—"coffee/or/tea," she says clearly—and when I reply "Neither," she understands immediately. "Could I have some orange juice instead?" I ask. She tells me that I can have orange juice *and* coffee or tea. Wow! Then I get a brilliant idea. "Could I have two orange juices?" She smiles a genuine smile. So do I. I'll bet no one ever took two orange juices in an airplane before.

Why I Really Hate Flying

So, here I sit, my omelet/and/veal/sausage framed by a glass of orange/juice on each side, feeling ever so individual. Can there be hope for flying after all?*

---

* Not for Louis. When he read this, he said: "By the way, I thought I was the only one who goes for two juices." So now I go for three.

16

HOPE FOR HUMANITY?

This is NOT the chapter about EMPOWERMENT. Empowerment is a gift from the gods, whereby a Management that does not understand the work cedes a bit of control over it to the workers who do. Empowerment is found in primitive organizations. In advanced organizations, such as beehives, the workers know what they have to do and just do it. This chapter closes our book on a hopeful note by describing an advanced act in a primitive place.

We are now arriving on Flight Whatchmacallit at Charlie the Gaul's Airport in Paris. As the plane comes to a screeching halt, we all leap up in unison, on cue, eager to become cattle again. Anything but sardines. All except me, who can't move because that meathead in front of me is fumbling for his trunk. Why can't he hurry up? Finally, mercifully, he extracts it, and I go for mine, only to be glared at by that other bonehead behind. What's the rush, buddy?

I can't wait to get out of the can, the big one. When I finally do, I discover to my horror that we have been herded into another can, one of those rectangular jobs. I wait by the front, lacing up my boxing gloves while we all get packed in, last of all the guy who went back for his coloring book. I wait while we shuttle, rattle, and roll, to be regurgitated into the terminal. I wait, somewhere up that wall, to wave my passport at the disinterested immigration official, so that I can wait to do my Samson Swing, so that I can wait to sneak my boxes of gold-plated gumdrops past the customs inspector, so that I can wait for the taxi that has been waiting for me.

Finally, I climb in and stretch out, reveling in my individuality, ecstatic in the knowledge that I am almost beyond their reach. We take off like a shot, whizzing past signs desperately trying to change my mind about consummate consumption, each one perfectly readable at several hundred kilometers an hour.

My excitement mounts in anticipation of what I seem to recall lies beyond. There is another world out there. I am sure of it.

Just then, off cue, a hand appears out of the car in front. It is holding a great big piece of paper, which it drops, with ever so casual determination, right there, on the perfectly formed asphalt. There is an insignia on the back of that car. It reads "Aeroports de Paris."

There *is* hope for humanity, even in the world of flying.

Coming soon—

from the same hysterical author:

Why I Hate Refilling the Stapler

(unless you can wait for his brilliant
collection of short stories entitled
Reflections from the Window)

We are sorry to have left you so little space for this.